E

LOC

MULT

COACHING STOCK

"The SPOTTERS COMPANION"

2013

35th Edition

Compiled by

The National Railway Enthusiasts Association

ISBN 978-0-906439-24-1

Published by NREA
(Email - Sales@nrea.org.uk)

Amended late February 2013

Produced by G B S Marketing, Worcester.

37194 pulls away from York with a test train 2Q88 Derby to Heaton on 14 June 2011.

(Cover Photo) Ron Cover

Codes

AD	Ashford (Hitachi class 395) EMUD
AF	Ashford Chart Leacon T&RSMD
AK	Ardwick, Manchester TMD
AL	Aylesbury TMD
AN	Allerton DMUD
AS	Allely's Haulage Yard, Studley
AW	Washwood Heath Boden Rail/Hanson Traction
AY	Ayr SD
AZ	Alizay, Euro Cargo Rail, France
BA	Basford Hall, Crewe
BC	Bicester MoD
BD	Birkenhead North T&RSMD
BF	Bedford Caudwell Walk EMUD
BH	Barrow Hill Roundhouse
BI	Brighton EMUD
BK	Bristol Barton Hill TMD
BM	Bournemouth T&RSMD
BN	Bounds Green T&RSMD
BO	Burton on Trent TMD (Nemesis Rail Ltd)
BQ	Bury East Lancs Railway
BS	Bescot TMD
BT	Bo'ness & Kinneil Railway
BY	Bletchley TMD
BZ	St Blazey (Par) T&RSMD
CA	Cambridge
CB	Midland Railway Centre, Butterley
CC	Clacton SD
CD	Crewe Diesel (storage)
CE	Crewe International Electric IEMD
CF	Cardiff Canton TMD/Pullman Rail(Colas)
CG	Crewe Gresty Lane TMD
CH	Chester TMD
CJ	Clapham SD
CK	Corkerhill SD
CO	Coquelles Eurotunnel IEMD (France)
CP	Crewe CARMD/Brook Sdgs
CQ	Crewe Heritage Centre T&RSMD
CS	Carnforth Steamtown T&RSMD (West Coast Railway Co. Ltd)
CY	Crewe South Yard
CZ	Central Rivers, Barton under Needwood
DE	East Dereham Mid Norfolk Railway
DF	Rail Vehicle Engineering, Derby
DL	Dollands Moor SD
DR	Doncaster SD/Wood Yard
DT	Didcot (DBS)
DW	Doncaster West Yard
DY	Derby Etches Park T&RSMD
EC	Edinburgh Craigentinny T&RSMD
EH	Eastleigh TMD
EM	East Ham EMUD
EN	Euston Downside CARMD
ER	Eurre TMD SNCF France
EX	Exeter St Davids DMUD
FD	Crewe Diesel (Freightliner)
FE	Crewe International (Freightliner)
FF	Forest - Midi T&RSMD (Brussels)
FP	Ferme Park Carriage Sidings
FR	Fratton SD
FX	Flexistowe Docks
GI	Gillingham EMUD
GW	Glasgow Shields Road TMD
HA	Haymarket TMD
HB	Horbury (Marcroft)
HE	Hornsey TMD
HG	Hither Green SD
HH	Keighley & Worth Valley Railway
HM	Healey Mills SD & WRD
HQ	New Traction on acceptance trials or stored loco/stock awaiting decision
HT	Heaton T&RSMD
IL	Ilford T&RSMD
IM	Immingham SD
IS	Inverness T&RSMD
KC	Carlisle Currock WRD
KM	Kingmoor Depot TMD, Carlisle
KR	Severn Valley Railway
KT	MoD Kineton
KY	Knottingley TMD
LA	Laira T&RSMD
LB	Loughborough Works (Wabtec)
LD	Leeds Midland Road TMD
LE	Landore T&RSMD
LH	LH Group Services, Barton under Needwood
LL	Liverpool Edge Hill CARMD
LM	Long Marston
LY	Le Landy, T&RSMD SNCF (Paris)
MA	Manchester Traincare Longsight

MD	Merehead TMD
MG	Margam LIP/Engineers Yard
MH	Millerhill SD
ML	Motherwell SD
MM	MoD Moreton in Marsh
MN	Machynlleth DMUD
MO	Mossend Yard
MQ	Meldon Quarry (Storage)
NC	Norwich Crown Point T&RSMD
NG	New Cross Gate CSD
NH	Newton Heath DMUD
NL	Neville Hill TMD
NM	Nottingham Eastcroft SD
NN	Northampton Kings Heath EMUD
NT	Northam EMUD (Southampton)
NY	North Yorkshire Moors Rly, Grosmont
OH	Old Oak Common EMUD
OO	Old Oak Common HST
OX	Oxford
OY	Midlands Traincare Centre (Oxley)
PC	Glasgow Traincare Centre (Polmadie)
PE	Peterborough Nene SD
PF	Peak Forest SD
PG	Peterborough SD
PM	St Philips Marsh T&RSMD
PN	Poznan, Euro Cargo Rail, Poland
PZ	Penzance T&RSMD
RD	Ruddington
RG	Reading DMUD
RL	Ropley (Mid Hants Railway)
RM	Ramsgate T&RSMD
RR	Doncaster Roberts Road (Hexthorpe)
RU	Rugby TMD
RY	Ryde (I.O.W.) EMUD
SA	Salisbury DMUD
SE	St Leonards T&RSMD
SG	Slade Green EMUD
SH	Southall Railway Centre CARMD
SJ	Stourbridge Junction
SK	Swanwick Jct, Midland Railway Butterley
SL	Stewarts Lane T&RSMD
SN	Shoeburyness SD or MOD Pigs Bay
SO	Soho TMD (Birmingham)
SP	Springs Branch (Wigan)
SU	Selhurst T&RSMD
SV	Wembley (Stonebridge Park)
SZ	Southampton Maritime TMD
TE	Tees Yard
TI	Temple Mills Eurostar T&RSMD
TJ	Tavistock Jct Yard (Colas Rail) SD
TM	Tyseley Locomotive Works
TO	Toton, EWS HQ, Diesel Locomotives
TS	Tyseley DMUD
TT	Toton Training Compound
TW	Toton WRD & Yards
TY	Tyne Yard
VW	Alstom HQ (Virgin West Coast)
WA	Warrington Arpley SD & Yards
WB	Wembley Traincare T&RSMD
WD	Wimbledon East EMUD
WE	Willesden Brent Sidings
WF	Wansford SD, Cambridgeshire
WH	Whatley (Mendip Workshop)
WN	Willesden Depot
WQ	EWS, stored awaiting decision
WR	West Ruslip SD
XW	Crofton, Wakefield (Bombardier)
YJ	Yeovil Junction
YK	National Railway Museum, York
ZA	Delta Rail/Rail Vehicle Engineering Limited
ZB	Wabtec Rail Limited Doncaster
ZC	Bombardier Transportation Crewe
ZD	Bombardier Transportation Derby CW
ZG	Eastleigh Works
ZH	Railcare Ltd Glasgow
ZI	Bombardier Transportation Ilford
ZJ	Turners/DB Axiom Rail-Stoke on Trent
ZK	Wabtec Rail Scotland, Kilmarnock
ZN	Railcare Ltd Wolverton
ZQ	Withdrawn Stock waiting disposal

CARMD	Carriage Maintenance Depot
CSD	Carriage Servicing Depot
D/EMUD	Diesel/Electric Multiple Unit Depot
IEMD	International Electric Maintenance Depot
SD	Servicing Depot
T & RSMD	Traction & Rolling Stock Maintenance Depot
TMD	Traction Maintenance Depot
WRD	Wagon Repair Depot

Note:- Locos shown HQ may have last known location shown e.g. (CD). At certain locations (e.g. BS), some locomotives are stored in nearby yards but are not shown as such because the situation is liable to change.

OPERATOR POOL CODES

ACAC	Various	AC Locomotive Group - Operational
ACXX	Various	AC Locomotive Group - Stored
ADFL	Various	Advenza Freight Locomotives (stored)
ATLO	Cl 08	Alstom Traincare Locomotives
ATXX	Various	Alstom Traincare Locomotives - long term repair
ATZZ	Various	Alstom Traincare Locomotives - waiting disposal
AWCA	Various	West Coast Railway Co. - Operational
AWCX	Various	West Coast Railway Co. - Non Operational/Stored
BREL	Cl 47	Boden Rail Engineering Ltd
CDJD	Cl 08	Serco Railtest Locomotives
CFOL	Various	Class 50 Operations Limited
COLO	Various	Colas Rail - Operational Locomotives
COLS	Various	Colas Rail - Stored Locomotives
CROL	Various	Cotswold Rail Engineering - Locomotives awaiting decision
DBLX	Cl 55	Deltic Preservation Society
DFEP	Cl 66	Freightliner - Locomotives, Poland
DFGC	Cl 86/5	Freightliner - Regeared trial loco
DFGH	Cl 70	Freightliner - Heavy Haul
DFGI	Cl 70	Freightliner - Intermodal traffic
DFGM	Cl 66/5	Freightliner - Intermodal traffic
DFHG	Cl 66	Freightliner - Heavy Haul, Modified General
DFHH	Cl 66/5 66/6	Freightliner - Heavy Haul
DFIM	Cl 66	Freightliner - Intermodal traffic, Modified
DFIN	Cl 66/5 66/9	Freightliner - Intermodal traffic, Low Emission Variant (SB)
DFLC	Cl 90	Freightliner - (Leased from SB)
DFLH	Cl 47	Freightliner - Heavy Haul
DFLS	Cl 08	Freightliner - General
DFNC	Cl 86/6	Freightliner - General
DFRT	Cl 66/5	Freightliner - Network Rail Infrastructure
DFTZ	Various	Freightliner - Locomotives off lease or on short term lease
DHLT	Various	Freightliner - Stored Locomotives
EFOO	Cl 57/6	First Great Western - (Leased from SB)
EFPC	Cl 43	First Great Western
EFSH	Cl 08	First Great Western
EHPC	Cl 43	CrossCountry (Arriva)
EJLO	Cl 08	London Midland - Locomotives
ELRD	Various	East Lancashire Railway - Diesels
EMPC	Cl 43	East Midlands Trains - (Leased from SB)
EMSL	Cl 08	East Midlands Trains - Shunting Locomotives
EMXX		East Midlands Trains - Miscellaneous
EPEX	Various	EuroPhoenix Locomotives - Export
EPUK	Various	EuroPhoenix Locomotives - UK

EPXS	Various	EuroPhoenix - Stored Locomotives
EPXX	Various	EuroPhoenix Locomotives - Unspecified
ETLO	Cl 86 & 87	Electric Traction Locomotives - Operational
ETLS	Cl 86	Electric Traction Locomotives - Stored
FAMT	Cl 37	Private Owner/Preserved
GBCM	Cl 66/7	GB Railfreight - General
GBED	Cl 73	GB Railfreight - Electro Diesel Locomotives (Hire)
GBEE	Cl 20	GB Railfreight - For Hire
GBET	Cl 92	GB Railfreight - Electric Traction
GBFM	Cl 66/7	GB Railfreight - (RETB equipped)
GBHL	Various	GB Railfreight - Locomotives hired out
GBNL	Cl66/7	GB Railfreight – Ex Netherlands
GBRT	Cl 66/7	GB Railfreight - Restricted Use
GBSD	Cl 66/7	GB Railfreight - Scottish Operation (RETB)
GBWM	Cl 08	GB Railfreight – Shunting Locomotives
GBZZ	Cl 73	GB Railfreight - Locomotives stored
GCHP	Cl 43	Grand Central Railway Company - HST
GPSS	Cl 08	Eurostar (UK) - EWS maintained
HBSH	Cl 08	Wabtec Rail Ltd, Doncaster - Leasing
HISE	Cl 08	Ex code for Maintrain Locos
HNRL	Various	Harry Needle Rail - Locomotives for hire
HNRS	Various	Harry Needle Rail - Stored Locomotives
HTLX	Various	Bars American Railway Services - Locomotives
HWSU	Cl 09	Southern
HYWD	Cl 73	South West Trains
IANA	Cl 90	Abellio Greater Anglia Ltd
IECA	Cl 91	East Coast
IECP	Cl 43	East Coast
KCSI	Cl 08	Adtranz (Bombardier) Ilford
KDSD	Cl 08	Adtranz (Bombardier) Doncaster
MBDL	Various	Private Owner/Preserved - Diesel Locos
MBED	Cl 73	Private Owner/Preserved - Electro-Diesel
MBEL	Various	Private Owner/Preserved - Electric Locos
MOLO	Cl 08	RT Rail Ltd - Hire Locomotives
MOLS	Cl 08	RT Rail Ltd - Stored Locomotives
MRLO	Various	Mainline Rail(BARS group) - Operational Locos
MRLS	Various	Mainline Rail(BARS group) - Stored Locos
MRSO	Cl 08	RMS Locotec(BARS group) - Hire Locomotives
MXXX	Various	Private Owner - not yet authorised to run on Network Rail
NRHL	Various	Nemesis Rail - Hire Locos
NRLO	Various	Nemesis Rail - Operational Locos
NRLS	Various	Nemesis Rail - Stored Locos
PTXX	Cl 92	Europorte 2 Locomotives (Eurotunnel)
QACL	Cl 86	Network Rail - AC Load Bank Locomotives
QADD	Various	Network Rail - Diesel Locos
QCAR	Cl 43	Network Rail - New Measurement Train
QETS	Cl 97/3	Network Rail - European Signalling

QSTR	Various	Network Rail - Stored Locomotives
QXXX	Various	Network Rail - Stored
RAJV	Various	Bo'ness & Kinneil Railway - Operational Locomotives
RCZH	Cl 08	Railcare Ltd, Glasgow
RCZN	Cl 08	Railcare Ltd, Wolverton
RFSH	Cl 08	Wabtec Rail Locomotives
RMSX	Cl08	RMS Locotec
RTLO	Cl 47	Riviera Trains - Locomotives Operational
RTLS	Cl 47	Riviera Trains - Locomotives Stored
RTSO	Cl 08	Riviera Trains - Shunting Locomotives Operational
RVLO	Various	Rail Vehicle Engineering, Derby - Locomotives Operational
RVLS	Various	Rail Vehicle Engineering, Derby - Stored
SAXL	Various	Eversholt Rail Group - Stored off lease, spare
SBXL	Various	Porterbrook Leasing Co Ltd - Stored off lease, spare
SCXL	Various	Angel Trains Leasing - Stored off lease, spare
TTLS	Various	Traditional Traction Locomotives
TTTC	Cl 37	Type 3 Traction Group
WAAN	Cl 67	D B Schenker - Network
WABN	Cl 67	D B Schenker - Network (RETB equipped)
WATN	Cl 67	D B Schenker - on hire to Arriva Trains
WAWN	Cl 67	D B Schenker - on hire to Chiltern Railways
WBAI	Cl 66	D B Schenker - Industrial
WBAK	Cl 66	D B Schenker - Construction
WBAL	Cl 66	D B Schenker - Logistics
WBBI	Cl 66	D B Schenker - Industrial (RETB equipped)
WBBK	Cl 66	D B Schenker - Construction (RETB equipped)
WBBL	Cl 66	D B Schenker - Logistics (RETB equipped)
WBEI	Cl 66	D B Schenker - Industrial (Euro Cargo Rail)
WBEN	Cl 66	D B Schenker - European Mods fitted (Euro Cargo Rail) France
WBEP	Cl 66	D B Schenker - European Mods fitted (Euro Cargo Rail) Poland
WBES	Cl 66	D B Schenker - Sandite (Euro Cargo Rail)
WBLI	Cl 66	D B Schenker - Industrial, Lickey Banker, auto coupler
WBSN	Various	D B Schenker – RHTT Duties/Sandite
WBST	Cl 66	D B Schenker - Sandite, trip cock fitted
WCAI	Cl 60	D B Schenker - Industrial 990 gallon fuel tanks
WCAK	Cl 60	D B Schenker - Construction 990 gallon fuel tanks
WCBI	Cl 60	D B Schenker - Industrial 1150 gallon fuel tanks
WCBK	Cl 60	D B Schenker - Construction 1150 gallon fuel tanks
WDAK	Cl 59/2	D B Schenker - Construction
WEFE	Cl 90	D B Schenker - Systemwide
WFMS	Various	D B Schenker - Fleet Management Unit, Holding Pool
WFMU	Various	D B Schenker - Fleet Management Unit Maintenance Pool
WNSO	Various	D B Schenker - Sold waiting collection
WNTR	Various	D B Schenker - Stored Tactical Reserve
WNTS	Various	D B Schenker - Stored Unserviceable
WNWX	Various	D B Schenker - Stored waiting or on Heavy Repair
WNYX	Cl 08/09	D B Schenker - Fleet Management Unit

WSSI	Cl 08/09	D B Schenker - Industrial
WSSK	Cl 08/09/66	D B Schenker - Construction
WSSL	Cl 08/09	D B Schenker - Logistics
WSXX	Cl 08	D B Schenker - Depot Pilot/internal user
WTAE	Cl 92	D B Schenker - Systemwide
WTEB	Cl 92	D B Schenker - Bulgaria
WTHE	Cl 92	D B Schenker - HS1 signal equipment fitted
WZFF	Cl 58	D B Schenker - Special Projects (hire to France)
WZKS	Cl 37	D B Schenker - Special Projects (hire to Spain)
WZTS	Various	D B Schenker - Contract Hire/Tactical Stored
XHAC	Various	Direct Rail Services - Operational Locos
XHCK	Cl 57	Direct Rail Services - Operational Locos
XHHP	Various	Direct Rail Services - Holding Pool
XHIM	Cl 66/4	Direct Rail Services - Intermodal
XHMW	Various	Direct Rail Services - Locos in main works/long term repairs
XHNC	Various	Direct Rail Services - Nuclear Traffic
XHND	Cl 37	Direct Rail Services - Infrastructure Monitoring
XHNR	Various	Direct Rail Services - Network Rail (sandite season only)
XHSS	Various	Direct Rail Services - Stored/Spares
XYPA	Cl 59/1	Mendip Rail (ARC) - (Maintained Merehead)
XYPO	Cl 59/0	Mendip Rail (Foster Yeoman)

Some locos may carry a name on one side only.

It must be noted that Locos, Units and Coaching Stock moved to scrap yards have generally been excluded in this publication although they may still be registered with Network Rail.

LOCOMOTIVES

CLASS 01/5

	Works No. & Builder	Name/No.	Built	Type	Owner	LOCATION
01507	RH459519	425 Venom	1961	0-6-0 DH	MBDL	Crossley Evans, Shipley
01508	RH466617	428	1961	0-6-0 DH	MBDL	ZG
01509	RH468043	433 Lesley	1963	0-6-0 DH	MBDL	AL
01510	TH320v	272	1987	0-4-0 DH	MoD	DM Eastriggs
01511	TH323v	275	1988	0-4-0 DH	MoD	DM Glen Douglas, Arrochar
01512	TH319v	301	1988	0-4-0 DH	MoD	DSDC Bicester
01513	TH318v	270	1987	0-4-0 DH	MoD	DSDC Bicester
01514	THv332	277	1988	0-4-0 DH	MoD	DM Glen Douglas, Arrochar
01515	TH321v	273	1987	0-4-0 DH	MoD	DM Glen Douglas, Arrochar
01520	TH322v	274	1987	0-4-0 DH	MoD	DSDC Bicester
01521	THv333	278	1988	0-4-0 DH	MoD	DSDC Bicester
01522	TH272v	254	1977	0-4-0 DH	MoD	Marchwood, Southampton
01523	TH299v	259	1981	0-4-0 DH	MoD	DSD Ashchurch
01524	TH301v	261	1982	0-4-0 DH	MoD	Ludgershall Railhead
01525	TH306v	264	1983	0-4-0 DH	MoD	DR Shoeburyness
01526	TH307v	265	1983	0-4-0 DH	MoD	DM Kineton, Warwickshire
01527	TH274v	266	1977	0-4-0 DH	MoD	Marchwood, Southampton
01528	TH309v	267	1984	0-4-0 DH	MoD	DR Shoeburyness
01529	TH310v	268	1984	0-4-0 DH	MoD	DM Longtown, Cumbria
01530	TH311v	269	1984	0-4-0 DH	MoD	DM Longtown, Cumbria
01541	TH300v	260	1982	0-4-0 DH	MoD	Marchwood, Southampton
01542	TH302v	262	1982	0-4-0 DH	MoD	DSD Ashchurch
01543	TH303v	263	1982	0-4-0 DH	MoD	DM Kineton
01544	TH270v	252	1977	0-4-0 DH	MoD	Marchwood, Southampton
01545	TH271v	253	1977	0-4-0 DH	MoD	DM Longtown, Cumbria
01546	TH273v	255	1977	0-4-0 DH	MoD	DM Kineton, Warwickshire
01547	TH308v	256	1983	0-4-0 DH	MoD	DM Kineton, Warwickshire
01548	TH275v	257	1978	0-4-0 DH	MoD	Ludgershall Railhead
01549	TH298v	258	1981	0-4-0 DH	MoD	Marchwood, Southampton
01550	TH324v	271	1987	0-4-0 DH	MoD	DSDC Bicester
01551	D1122	Lancelot	1966	0-4-0 DH	MBDL	AK
01552	TH167v		1966	0-6-0 DH	MBDL	LM
01555	TH292v	8 James	1980	0-6-0 DH	MBDL	TJ Thomson, Stockton
01562	TH257v	Black Beast	1975	0-6-0 DH	MBDL	Croft Quarry
01563	BR Derby	12083	1950	0-6-0 DE	MBDL	Battlefield Steam Railway
01564	BR Derby	12088	1951	0-6-0 DE	MBDL	Widdrington Opencast Quarry
01565	S10144		1963	0-6-0 DH	MBDL	Booths, Rotherham
01566	BR Swindon	D9504	1964	0-6-0 DH	MBDL	Nene Valley Railway
01567	TH276v	Elizabeth	1978	0-4-0 DH	MBDL	TJ Thomson, Stockton

01568*	TH264v	Helen	1976	0-4-0 DH	MBDL	TJ Thomson, Stockton
01569	TH281v	Emma	1978	0-4-0 DH	MBDL	TJ Thomson, Stockton
01570	HB773	Blue John	1990	B-B DH	MBDL	CE
01571	TH261v	Coral	1976	0-6-0 DH	MBDL	Bugle, Cornwall
01572*	RR10256	Kathryn	1968	0-6-0 DH	MBDL	Croft Quarry
01573	HE6294	HL006	1965	0-6-0 DH	MBDL	Cobra Railfreight, Middlesbrough
01583	RH459517	Valiant	1961	0-6-0 DH	MBDL	Lavender Line, East Sussex
01585	RH459518	Scaz	1961	0-6-0 DH	MBDL	Chiltern Railways, Wembley

Builders codes: AB - Andrew Barclay. BR - British Railways. H - Hunslett Engine Company.
RH - Ruston & Hornsby. RR - Rolls Royce. S - Sentinel. TH - Thomas Hill.
*01568 renumbered from 01554. *01572 renumbered from 01561.

CLASS 03 BRITISH RAIL SHUNTER 0-6-0

Built: 1962
Weight: 31 tonnes
Maximum Tractive Effort: 15,300 lbf
Transmission: Mechanical

Maximum Speed: 28 mph
Engine: Gardner 204 hp
Wheel Diameter: 1092 mm
Route Availability: 1

03179	Clive	MBDL	Hornsey Depot only

CLASS 07 RUSTON & HORNSBY SHUNTER 0-6-0

Built: 1962
Weight: 42 tonnes
Maximum Tractive Effort: 28,240 lbf
Transmission: Electric. AEI Traction Motor

Maximum Speed: 20 mph
Engine: Paxman 6-cyl RPHL
Wheel Diameter: 1067 mm
Route Availability: 6

07007	(2991)	MBDL	ZG
07013	(2997)	HNRS	BH

CLASS 08 BRITISH RAIL SHUNTER 0-6-0

Built: 1955-62
Weight: 50 tonnes
Maximum Tractive Effort: 35,000 lbf
Transmission: Two English Electric Traction Motors

Maximum Speed: 15/20 mph
Engine: English Electric 400 hp
Wheel Diameter: 1372 mm
Route Availability: 5

•reduced cab height, *train air brake only, all others dual braked
+ multiple working fitted. b buckeye coupler fitted.

08077	DHLT	LHs
08308*	MRSO	IS
08375*	MRSO	Teesport
08389•b	HNRS	BO
08393		LHs
08401	MBDL	Boulby
08405*	WNYX	CE
08410*	EFSH	PZ
08411	TTLS	Colne Valley
08417*	QADD	ZA
08428•b	WNYX	CE
08441•b	TTLS	FX
08442*‡	i/user	EH
08445	MBDL	Daventry
08451‡	ATZZ	MA
08454	ATLO	MA
08460	TTLS	Colne Valley
08472*	RFSH	EC
08480*	WNYX	TO
08483*‡	EFSH	OO
08484*‡	TTLS	Toddington
08495‡	WSSK	EH
08499*	WSXX	CF
08500*	WNYX	TE
08502	HNRL	BH
08503	HNRS	Wishaw
08507*	HNRL	Boston
08511•b	TTLS	FX
08516*‡	i/user	BK
08523	MRSO	Wolsingham
08525‡	EMSL	NL
08527	HNRL	Scunthorpe
08530	DFLS	SZ
08531*	DFLS	Tilbury
08536	HISE	DF
08567*	WNYX	CE
08568*‡	RCZH	ZH
08571*	HBSH	BN
08573	MRSO	ZI
08575	DHLT	SZ
08578•b	WNXX	TO
08580	WNXX	BS
08585*‡	DFLS	FX
08588	MRSO	AW
08593•b	WNXX	CE
08596*	RFSH	BN
08605	WSSK	Mountsorrel
08611	ATLO	MA
08613	MBDL	Onllwyn
08615	RFSH	EC
08616‡	EJLO	TS
08617	ATLO	SV
08623	WSSL	Hams Hall
08624	DFLS	Trafford Park
08629	RCZN	ZN
08630*	WNXX	TT
08632	WSSK	TO
08633*	WSSK	Westbury
08641	EFSH	LA
08643	MBDL	Merehead
08644	EFSH	LA
08645‡	EFSH	LB
08648‡	MRSO	Teesport
08649	RCZN	ZN
08653	WNXX	TT
08663*‡	EFSH	PM
08669*‡	RFSH	ZB
08670*	TTLS	Colne Valley
08676	WSSL	MO
08678‡	AWCX	CS
08682‡	KDSD	ZA
08683	TTLS	Colne Valley
08685	HNRS	BH
08690‡	EMSL	NL
08691‡	DFLS	LH
08696*	ATLO	Polmadie
08697	EMSL	ZA
08699	MBDL	Shotton
08701*	WNXX	TT
08703•b	WNYX	DR
08704	HNRL	BQ
08706•b	WNYX	CE
08709	WNXX	BS
08711b	WNXX	TE
08714	WSXX	Marcroft Stoke
08721‡	ATLO	LL
08724	HBSH	ZB
08730‡	RCZH	ZH
08735•b	WNYX	EH
08737•b	WSSI	MG
08738+	WNTS	TT
08742	WSSK	Hoo Jct
08743	MBDL	Wilton
08750	MRSO	Ketton
08752	WSSK	DT
08754	RMSX	NC
08756	MRSO	Shotton
08757	WNYX	DT
08762	MRSO	Washwood
08765	HNRS	BO
08780	RTSO	SH
08782*‡	WSSK	DR
08784	WNTS	TO
08785*	DFLS	SZ
08786*	HNRS	BH
08788	MRSO	IS
08790‡	ATLO	OY
08795	EFSH	LE
08799*‡	WNYX	CE
08802	WSSK	DR
08804	WNYX	CE
08805‡	EJLO	SO
08809*	MRSO	AW
08810*	MBDL	HT
08818‡	HNRL	Scunthorpe
08822‡	EFSH	PM
08824•b	WSXX	CE
08830	MBDL	CQ
08834	HNRL	CG
08836	EFSH	OO

Loco	Pool	Location
08847	MRSO	NC
08850	MBDL	NY
08853*	RFSH	ZB
08865	WSSK	BS
08868	MBDL	CP
08870	MBDL	Wolsingham
08871	MBDL	Teesport
08873	DFLS	SZ
08874‡	MRSO	AS
08877	WSXX	SP
08879	WNYX	CE
08886	WNXX	CE
08887*	ATZZ	SV
08888*	WSSI	IM
08891	DHLT	LH
08892	HNRL	BO
08899*	EMSL	DY
08903	MBDL	Wilton
08904	WNYX	CE
08905b	HNRS	Hope
08907*	WSSK	Hoo Jct
08908‡	EMSL	NL
08913	MBDL	Daventry FLT
08918	HNRS	BO
08922	WNTS	TO
08924	HNRS	BH
08925	GBWM	Whitemoor
08934*	GBWM	Cardiff Tidal
08936	MBDL	Shotton
08939b+	WNTS	TT
08943	HNRL	CZ
08947*	MBDL	Isle of Grain
08948	GPSS	TI
08950*‡	EMSL	NL
08954	HNRL	BO
08956	CDJD	Asfordby
08993	WNTS	DR
08994*b	WNTS	TO
08995*	WSSK	MO

Note: 08480 shows TOTON No. 1 on sides. 08588 carries number 17. 08616 shows 3783 on sides. 08682 carries number D3849. 08701 shows TYNE 100 on sides. 08824 shows IEMD01 on sides.

08405/495/578/596/632/706/735/742/752/782/784/802/804/886/888 have remote control fitted
08507 has a barcode type number 9870 0008 507-4

‡ 08442	Richard J Wenham Eastleigh Depot December 1989 - July 1999
‡ 08451	M A SMITH
‡ 08483	DUSTY Driver David Miller
‡ 08484	CAPTAIN NATHANIEL DARELL
‡ 08495	NOEL KIRTON OBE
‡ 08516	RORY
‡ 08525	DUCAN BEDFORD
‡ 08568	St. Rollox
‡ 08585	Vicky
‡ 08616	TYSELEY 100
‡ 08645	Mike Baggott
‡ 08648	Old Geoff
‡ 08663	Jack
‡ 08669	Bob Machin
‡ 08678	ARTILLA
‡ 08682	Lionheart
‡ 08690	DAVID THIRKILL
‡ 08691	Terri
‡ 08721	DOWNHILL C.S.
‡ 08730	The Caley
‡ 08782	CASTLETON WORKS
‡ 08790	Steve Purser
‡ 08799	FRED
‡ 08805	CONCORDE
‡ 08818	MOLLY
‡ 08822	John
‡ 08874	Catherine
‡ 08908	IVAN STEPHENSON
‡ 08950	DAVID LIGHTFOOT

Bombardier shunters not registered for Network Rail lines:- 003(08846) ZD, 004(08602) BOMBER ZD,

CLASS 09 BRITISH RAIL SHUNTER 0-6-0

Built: 1959-62
Weight: 50 tonnes
Maximum Tractive Effort: 25,000 lbf
Transmission: Two English Electric Traction Motors
Maximum Speed: 27 mph
Engine: English Electric 400 hp
Wheel Diameter: 1372 mm
Route Availability: 5

*train air brake only, b buckeye coupler fitted

09002	GBWM	Whitemoor Yd	09009	GBWM	Barton Dock	09019	HNRL	BO
09006	WNXX	DR	09014	HNRS	BO	09024	WNSO	Wishaw
09007	MBDL	WN	09018	HNRL	Hope	09026*	HWSU	BI

09026 Cedric Wares.

09/1 & 09/2 Converted 08 regeared and maximum speed increased to 27mph

09106	WSSK	WA	09201*b	WNYX	CE	09204*b	MBDL	CP

CLASS 20 ENGLISH ELECTRIC TYPE 1 Bo-Bo

Built: 1957-68
Weight: 73-76 tonnes
Maximum Tractive Effort: 42,000 lbf
Transmission: Four English Electric Traction Motors
Maximum Speed: 60-75 mph
Engine: English Electric 1000 hp
Wheel Diameter: 1092 mm
Route Availability: 5/6

20016	HNRS	LM	20088	HNRS	LM	20142	GBEE	WR
20020	RAJV	BT	20092	HNRS	LM	20166	HNRS	Wensleydale
20035	TTLS	Colne Valley	20096	GBEE	BH	20168	HNRL	Hope
20056	HNRL	Scunthorpe	20107	GBEE	BH	20188	MBDL	AW
20057	HNRS	BH	20118	HNRL	BH	20189	GBEE	WR
20063	TTLS	Shackerstone	20121	HNRS	Wensleydale	20227	GBEE	WR
20066	HNRL	Scunthorpe	20132	HNRL	BH	20228	TTLS	Barry
20081	HNRS	LM						

20132 Barrow Hill Depot.. 20166 River Fowey. 20168 SIR GEORGE EARLE.
20227 SIR JOHN BETJEMAN.

20056 carries No. 81. 20066 carries No. 82.

20/3 & 20/9 Owned by Direct Rail Services Ltd (British Nuclear Fuels)

All air brake only

20/3 refurbished 1995-1998 from 20047/084/127/120/095/187/075/102/042/117/104

20/9 refurbished 1989 from 20101/083/041/225/219

20301	XHSS	ZG	20309	XHSS	KM	20901	GBEE	BH
20302	XHSS	ZG	20311	GBEE	BH	20903	HNRS	BO
20303	XHSS	ZG	20312	XHNC	KM	20904	HNRS	BO
20304	XHSS	ZG	20314	GBEE	BH	20905	GBEE	BH
20305	XHSS	CG	20315	XHSS	KM	20906	HNRL	BH
20308	XHNC	KM						

20301 Max Joule 1958-1999. 20305 Gresty Bridge. 20314 Vulcan Foundry. 20905 Roger Whip. 20314 has a barcode type number 92700020314-5. 20906 carries No. 3.

CLASS 25 BRITISH RAIL/SULZER TYPE 2 BO-BO

Built: 1965
Weight: 72 tonnes
Maximum Tractive Effort: 45,000 lbf
Transmission: Four AEI Traction Motors
Maximum Speed: 60 mph
Engine: Sulzer 1250 hp
Wheel Diameter: 1143 mm
Route Availability: 5

D7628(25278)	MBDL	NY	SYBILIA

CLASS 26 BIRMINGHAM RAILWAY CARRIAGE & WAGON Co LTD TYPE 3 BO-BO

Built: 1958-59
Weight: 72 tonnes
Maximum Tractive Effort: 42,000lbf
Transmission: Four Crompton-Parkinson Traction Motors
Maximum Speed: 75 mph
Engine: Sulzer 1160hp
Wheel Diameter: 1092mm
Route Availability:

26004(D5304)	RAJV	BT	26024(D5324)	RAJV	BT

CLASS 27 BIRMINGHAM RAILWAY CARRIAGE & WAGON Co LTD TYPE 3 BO-BO

Built: 1961
Weight: 72 tonnes
Maximum Tractive Effort: 40,000 lbf
Transmission: Four GEC Traction Motors

Maximum Speed: 90 mph
Engine: Sulzer 1250 hp
Wheel Diameter: 1092mm
Route Availability:

27001(D5347)	RAJV	BT	27005(D5351)	RAJV	BT

CLASS 31 BRUSH TYPE 2 AIA-AIA

Built: 1957-1962
Weight: 107-113 tonnes
Maximum Tractive Effort: 36,000 lbf
Transmission: Four Brush Traction Motors

Maximum Speed: 60-90 mph
Engine: English Electric 1470 hp
Wheel Diameter: 1092mm(Driven)
1003 mm(Centre)
Route Availability: 5 or 6

31/1 # vacuum brake isolated/removed. (31190 carries number D5613)

31105	QADD	ZA	31190	HTLX	AW	31285	QADD	ZA
31106#	RVLO	ZA	31233#	QADD	ZA	31289	NRLS	HQ
31128	NRLO	NY						

31128 CHARYBDIS.

31/4 Fitted Eth or 31/6 Eth isolated # vacuum brake isolated/removed

31422	MRLS	ZA	31459	RVLO	ZA	31468	MRLO	Wolsingham
31452	HTLX	DF	31461	NRLO	BO	31601	HTLX	AW
31454	HTLX	Wolsingham	31465	QADD	ZA	31602	HTLX	AW

31459 CERBERUS. 31468 HYDRA.

CLASS 33 BIRMINGHAM RAILWAY CARRIAGE & WAGON Co LTD TYPE 3 Bo-Bo

Built: 1960-2 **Maximum Speed:** 60-85 mph
Weight: 78-79 tonnes **Engine:** Sulzer 1550 hp
Maximum Tractive Effort: 45,000 lbf **Wheel Diameter:** 1092mm
Transmission: Four Crompton-Parkinson Traction Motors **Route Availability:** 6
Vacuum brake isolated/removed

33/0

33012	MBDL	Swanage	33021	NRLS	Churnet Valley	33029#	AWCA	CS
33019#	NRLS	Shackerstone	33025	AWCX	SH	33030	AWCX	CS

33019 Griffon. 33021 Captain Charles. 33025 Glen Falloch. 33029 Glen Loy.
33012 carries number D6515.

33/1 Equipped for multiple working with EMU,TC stock and Class 73

33103 NRLO Bluebell Rly

33103 SWORDFISH. 33109(D6525) Captain Bill Smith RNR.

33/2 Built to former Hastings line loading guage

33207 AWCA CS Jim Martin

CLASSES 37 ENGLISH ELECTRIC TYPE 3 Co-Co

Built: 1960-65 **Maximum Speed:** 80/90 mph
Weight: 102-120 tonnes **Engine:** English Electric 1,750 hp
Maximum Tractive Effort: 55,500-62,680 lbf **Wheel Diameter:** 1092mm
Transmission: Six English Electric Traction Motors **Route Availability:** 5 or 7
* extended range fuel tanks fitted # vacuum brake isolated/removed

37/0

37023	XHMW	AS	37069#*	XHSS	CG	37214	AWCX	CS
37025	RAJV	BT	37165#*	MBDL	CSs	37218*	XHNC	KM
37038	XHNC	KM	37175	RAJV	BT	37229	XHSS	KM
37057*	HNRL	BH	37194	XHNC	KM	37259	XHNC	KM
37059#*	XHSS	BH	37198*	MBDL	Quorn	37261#*	XHNC	KM

37263	MBDL	TM	37275	MBDL	BH	37350	MBDL	YK
37264	FAMT	TM	37308*	CFOL	Dean Forest			

37025 Inverness TMD. 37175 W.S. Sellar. 37214 Loch Laidon. 37229 Jonty Jarvis 8-12-1998 to 18-3-2005.

37/4 fitted Eth & twin fuel tanks

37401	XHHP	KM (BH)	
37402	XHHP	KM (CG)	
37403	RAJV	BT	
37405	XHHP	KM (CG)	
37407	FAMT	Churnet Valley	
37409#	XHAC	KM	Lord Hinton
37413	FAMT	BO	
37419	XHAC	KM	Carl Haviland 1954-2012
37422	XHHP	KM	
37423	XHND	KM	Spirit of the Lakes
37424	FAMT	Churnet Valley	
37425	XHAC	KM	

37/5 Refurbished with alternator replacing the main generator, regeared bogies & twin fuel tanks fitted.

(37601 - 37612 air brake only, TDM fitted, Max speed 90 mph reclassified 37/6)

37503	HNRL	BHs	37605	XHND	KM	37668		CSs
37510#	XHSS	KM (BH)	37606	XHNC	KM	37669#	AWCX	CS
37516	AWCA	CS	37607	XHNC	KM	37670	HNRS	Kingsbury
37517#		CSs	37608	XHNC	KM	37676#	AWCA	CS
37518	MBDL	BQ	37609	XHNC	KM	37679	FAMT	BO
37521	HNRL	BH	37610	XHND	KM	37682	XHNC	KM
37601	XHNC	KM	37611	XHNC	KM	37685#	AWCA	CS
37602	XHNC	KM	37612	XHNC	KM	37688	XHND	KM
37603	XHND	KM	37667	XHND	KM			
37604	XHND	KM						

37518 Fort William/An Gearasdan. 37601 Class 37 – Fifty. 37610 T.S. (Ted) Cassady 14.5.61 - 6.4.08. 37676 Loch Rannoch. 37685 Loch Arkaig. 37688 Kingmoor TMD.

37/7 Refurbished with alternator replacing the main generator, regeared bogies, twin fuel tanks, ballast weights added.

37703#	WZKS	DL	37712#	AWCX	CS	37716#	WZKS	DL
37706	AWCA	CS	37714#	WZKS	DL	37718#	WZKS	DL
37710		CSs						

97/3 Refurbished 37 for Network Rail on European Rly Traffic Management System

97301 37100	QETS	ZA		97303 37178	QETS	ZA	
97302 37170	QETS	ZA		97304 37217	QETS	ZA	John Tiley

Class 40 English Electric Type 4 1Co-Co1

Built: 1958-62 **Maximum Speed:** 90 mph
Weight: 131-136 tonnes **Engine:** English Electric 2,000 hp
Maximum Tractive Effort: 52,000 lbf **Wheel Diameter:** 1143 mm, 914 mm
Transmission: Six English Electric Traction Motors **Route Availability:** 6

40013	HNRS	BH		40135 (D335)	ELRD	BQ	
40122	MBDL	YK		40145 (D345)	ELRD	BQ	East Lancashire Railway

Class 43 HST Power Cars Bo-Bo

Built: 1976-82 **Maximum Speed:** 125 mph
Weight: 70 tonnes **Engine:** MTU 4000, *Paxman VP 185
Maximum Tractive Effort: 17,980 lbf **Wheel Diameter:** 1020 mm
Route Availability: 5
Transmission: Brush Traction Motors or GEC Traction Motors

43002	EFPC	LA		43021	EFPC	LA	David Austin-Cartoonist
43003	EFPC	LA	ISAMBARD KINGDOM BRUNEL	43022	EFPC	LA	
43004	EFPC	LA	First for the future/ First ar gyfer y dyfodol	43023	EFPC	LA	
43005	EFPC	LA		43024	EFPC	LA	Great Western Society 1961-2011 Didcot Railway Centre
43009	EFPC	LA	First transforming travel				
43010	EFPC	LA		43025	EFPC	LA	The Institution of Railway Operators 2000-2010 TEN YEARS PROMOTING OPERATIONAL EXCELLENCE
43012	EFPC	LA					
43013	QCAR	EC					
43014	QCAR	EC					
43015	EFPC	LA		43026	EFPC	LA	
43016	EFPC	LA		43027	EFPC	LA	Glorious Devon
43017	EFPC	LA		43028	EFPC	LA	
43018	EFPC	LA		43029	EFPC	LA	
43020	EFPC	LA	MTU Power, Passion, Partnership	43030	EFPC	LA	Christian Lewis Trust

43031	EFPC	LA	
43032	EFPC	LA	
43033	EFPC	LA	Driver Brian Cooper 15 June 1947- 5 October 1999
43034	EFPC	LA	TravelWatch SouthWest
43035	EFPC	LA	
43036	EFPC	LA	
43037	EFPC	LA	PENYDARREN
43040	EFPC	LA	Bristol St. Phillips Marsh
43041	EFPC	OO	Meningitis Trust Support for Life
43042	EFPC	OO	
43043*	EMPC	NL	
43044*	EMPC	NL	
43045*	EMPC	NL	
43046*	EMPC	NL	
43047*	EMPC	NL	
43048*	EMPC	NL	T.C.B. Miller MBE
43049*	EMPC	NL	Neville Hill
43050*	EMPC	NL	
43052*	EMPC	NL	
43053	EFPC	LE	University of Worcester
43054*	EMPC	NL	The Sheffield Star 125 Years
43055*	EMPC	NL	
43056x	EFPC	LE	The Royal British Legion
43058*	EMPC	NL	
43059*	EMPC	NL	
43060*	EMPC	NL	
43061*	EMPC	NL	
43062	QCAR	EC	John Armitt
43063	EFPC	OO	
43064*	EFPC	NL	
43066*	EFPC	NL	
43069	EFPC	OO	
43070	EFPC	OO	The Corps of Royal Electrical and Mechanical Engineers
43071	EFPC	OO	
43073*	EFPC	NL	
43075*	EFPC	NL	
43076*	EFPC	NL	IN SUPPORT OF HELP for HEROES
43078	EFPC	OO	
43079	EFPC	OO	
43081*	EFPC	NL	
43082*	EFPC	NL	RAILWAY children, THE VOICE FOR STREET CHILDREN WORLDWIDE

43083*	EMPC	NL	
43086	EFPC	OO	
43087	EFPC	OO	11 Explosive Ordnance Disposal Regiment Royal Logistic Corps
43088	EFPC	OO	
43089*	EMPC	NL	
43091	EFPC	OO	
43092	EFPC	OO	
43093	EFPC	OO	
43094	EFPC	OO	
43097	EFPC	OO	Environment Agency
43098	EFPC	OO	
43122	EFPC	OO	
43124	EFPC	LE	
43125	EFPC	LE	
43126	EFPC	LE	
43127	EFPC	LE	Sir Peter Parker 1924-2002 Cotswold Line 150
43128	EFPC	LE	
43129	EFPC	LE	
43130	EFPC	LE	
43131	EFPC	LE	
43132	EFPC	LE	We Save the Children - Will You?
43133	EFPC	LE	
43134	EFPC	LE	
43135	EFPC	LE	
43136	EFPC	LE	
43137	EFPC	LE	Newton Abbot 150
43138	EFPC	LE	
43139	EFPC	LE	Driver Stan Martin 25 June 1950 - 6 November 2004
43140	EFPC	LE	
43141	EFPC	LE	
43142	EFPC	LE	Reading Panel Signal Box 1965-2010
43143	EFPC	LE	Stroud 700
43144	EFPC	LE	
43145	EFPC	LE	
43146	EFPC	LE	
43147	EFPC	LE	
43148	EFPC	LE	
43149	EFPC	LE	University of Plymouth
43150	EFPC	LE	
43151	EFPC	LE	
43152	EFPC	LE	
43153	EFPC	OO	

43154	EFPC	OO	
43155	EFPC	OO	
43156	EFPC	OO	Dartington International Summer School
43158	EFPC	OO	
43159	EFPC	OO	
43160	EFPC	OO	Sir Moir Lockhead OBE
43161	EFPC	OO	
43162	EFPC	OO	
43163	EFPC	OO	Exeter Panel Signal Box 21st Anniversary 2009
43164	EFPC	OO	
43165	EFPC	OO	Prince Michael of Kent
43168	EFPC	OO	
43169	EFPC	OO	THE NATIONAL TRUST
43170	EFPC	OO	
43171	EFPC	OO	
43172	EFPC	OO	
43174	EFPC	OO	
43175	EFPC	OO	GWR 175 ANNIVERSARY
43176	EFPC	OO	
43177	EFPC	OO	
43179	EFPC	OO	Pride of Laira
43180	EFPC	OO	
43181	EFPC	OO	
43182	EFPC	OO	
43183	EFPC	OO	
43185	EFPC	OO	Great Western
43186	EFPC	OO	
43187	EFPC	OO	
43188	EFPC	OO	
43189	EFPC	OO	RAILWAY HERITAGE TRUST
43190	EFPC	OO	
43191	EFPC	OO	
43192	EFPC	OO	
43193	EFPC	OO	
43194	EFPC	OO	
43195	EFPC	OO	
43196	EFPC	OO	
43197	EFPC	OO	
43198	EFPC	OO	Oxfordshire 2007
43206	IECP	EC	
43207	EHPC	EC	
43208	IECP	EC	Lincolnshire Echo
43238	IECP	EC	
43239	IECP	EC	
43251	IECP	EC	
43257	IECP	EC	
43272	IECP	EC	
43274	IECP	EC	
43277	IECP	EC	
43285	EHPC	EC	
43290	IECP	EC	mtu - fascination of power
43295	IECP	EC	
43296	IECP	EC	
43299	IECP	EC	
43300	IECP	EC	Craigentinny
43301	EHPC	EC	
43302	IECP	EC	
43303	EHPC	EC	
43304	EHPC	EC	
43305	IECP	EC	
43306	IECP	EC	
43307	IECP	EC	
43308	IECP	EC	
43309	IECP	EC	
43310	IECP	EC	
43311	IECP	EC	
43312	IECP	EC	
43313	IECP	EC	
43314	IECP	EC	
43315	IECP	EC	
43316	IECP	EC	
43317	IECP	EC	
43318	IECP	EC	
43319	IECP	EC	
43320	IECP	EC	
43321	EHPC	EC	
43357	EHPC	EC	
43366	EHPC	EC	
43367	IECP	EC	DELTIC 50 1955-2005
43378	EHPC	EC	
43384	GCHP	HT	
43423	GCHP	HT	VALENTA 1972-2010
43465	GCHP	HT	
43467	GCHP	HT	
43468	GCHP	HT	
43480	GCHP	HT	
43484	GCHP	HT	PETER FOX 1942-2011 PLATFORM 5

43206-208/238/239/251/257/272/274/277/285/290/295/296/299-321/357/366/367/378/384/423/465/467/468/480/484 renumbered from 43006-008/038/039/051/057/072/074/077/085/090/095/096/099-121/157/166/167/178/184/123/065/067/068/080/084

CLASS 47 BRITISH RAIL & BRUSH TYPE 4 Co-Co

Built: 1963-67
Weight: 117-125 tonnes
Maximum Tractive Effort: 60,000 lbf
Transmission: Six Brush Traction Motors

Maximum Speed: 75-100 mph
Engine: Sulzer 2580 hp
Wheel Diameter: 1143 mm
Route Availability: 6 or 7

47/0 built with boiler # vacuum brake isolated/removed x sandite fitted
+ fitted with multiple working equipment *extended range fuel tanks fitted

47194*	AWCX	CS	
47236*		CSs	
47237+*	AWCA	CS	
47245#+*	AWCA	CS	
47270#*	AWCA	CS	SWIFT (also carries number D1971)

47/3 built without train heat # vacuum brake isolated/removed, x sandite fitted
* extended range fuel tanks. + fitted with multiple working equipment.

47355#+*	AWCX	CS	
47368		CSs	
47375#*	NRLO	BO	TINSLEY TRACTION DEPOT

47/4 electric train heat † max speed restricted to 75mph
* extended range fuel tanks fitted. + multiple working fitted

47484	TTLS	Wishaw	(at Goodmans Yard)
47488#	NRLS	BO	
47492	AWCX	CS	
47500	AWCA	CS	
47501	XHAC	KM	Craftsman
47526		CSs	
47580	MBDL	TM	County of Essex
47640	NRLS	BO	(at Shackerstone)
47643	RAJV	BT	

47/7 push-pull & extended range fuel tanks fitted **Max speed 100 mph**

47703	HNRL	BO	
47712	XHSS	CP	Pride of Carlisle
47714+	HNRL	Asfordby	

47/7 Rail Express Systems fitted with extended range fuel tanks and for operation with propelling control vehicles # vacuum brake isolated/removed. + multiple working fitted

47727#+	COLO	AW	Rebecca
47739#+	COLO	AW	Robin of Templecombe
47744#	NRLS	BO	

47746# AWCX CS
47747# XHHP CG
47749#+ COLO AW Demelza
47760# AWCA CS
47768 AWCX CS
47769# RTLO CP Resolve
47772 AWCX CS
47773 MBDL TM (also carries number D1755)
47776 AWCX CS
47786# AWCA CS Roy Castle OBE
47787# AWCX CS Windsor Castle
47790#+ XHAC KM Galloway Princess

47/4 extended range fuel tanks fitted except 47798/804
vacuum brake isolated/removed . +multiple working fitted

47798# MBDL YK Prince William
47802 XHAC KM Pride of Cumbria
47804# AWCA CS
47805#+ XHAC KM
47810# XHAC KM Peter Bath MBE 1927-2006
47811# DFLH BAs
47812#+ RTLO CP (also carries number D1916)
47813#+ XHAC KM Solent
47815#+ RTLO CP GREAT WESTERN (also carries number D1748)
47816# DFLH BAs
47818# XHAC KM
47826# AWCA CS
47828#+ XHAC KM
47830# DFLH BHs
47832# XHNC KM Solway Princess
47839#+ XHHP ZG
47841# XHAC KM
47843#+ RTLO CP VULCAN
47847#+ RTLO CDs
47848#+ RTLO CP TITAN STAR
47851# AWCA CS
47853#+ XHAC KM RAIL EXPRESS
47854# AWCA CS Diamond Jubilee

Class 50 ENGLISH ELECTRIC TYPE 4 Co-Co

Built: 1967/68
Weight: 117 tonnes
Maximum Tractive Effort: 48,500 lbf
Transmission: 6 English Electric Traction Motors
Maximum Speed: restricted to 90 mph
Engine: English Electric 2700 hp
Wheel Diameter: 1092 mm
Route Availability: 6

50026	CFOL	AW	Indomitable
50031	CFOL	KR	Hood
50035	CFOL	KR	Ark Royal
50044	CFOL	KR	EXETER
50049	CFOL	KR	Defiance

50031/044/049 carry numbers D431/444/449. 50035 carries number 50135.

Class 52 BRITISH RAILWAYS TYPE 4 C-C

Built: 1963
Weight: 108 tonnes
Maximum Tractive Effort: 66,700 lbf
Transmission: Hydraulic
Maximum Speed: restricted to 90 mph
Engine: 2 x Maybach MD655 1500 hp
Wheel Diameter: 1092 mm
Route Availability: 6

D1015	MBDL	HQ	WESTERN CHAMPION

D1062 WESTERN COURIER ✓

CLASS 55 ENGLISH ELECTRIC TYPE 5 (DELTIC) Co-Co

Built: 1961/62
Weight: 105 tonnes
Maximum Tractive Effort: 50,000 lbf
Transmission: 6 English Electric Traction Motors
Maximum Speed: 100 mph
Engine: 2 Napier-Deltic x 1650 hp
Wheel Diameter: 1092 mm
Route Availability: 5

55002		MBDL	YK	THE KING'S OWN YORKSHIRE LIGHT INFANTRY
55009	D9009	DBLX	BQ	ALYCIDON
55015		DBLX	BH	TULYAR
55016		MBDL	BQ	GORDON HIGHLANDER
55019		DBLX	BH	ROYAL HIGHLAND FUSILIER
55022	D9000	ELRD	BQ	ROYAL SCOTS GREY

CLASS 56 BRITISH RAIL & BRUSH TYPE 5 Co-Co

Built: 1976-1984 **Maximum Speed:** 80 mph
Weight: 125 tonnes **Engine:** Rushton-Paxman 3250 hp
Maximum Tractive Effort: 61,800 lbf **Wheel Diameter:** 1143 mm
Transmission: Six Brush Traction Motors **Route Availability:** 7
56007/09/018 built by Electroputere at Craiova, Roumania sub contracting to Brush

56007	NRHL	BO		56091	HTLX	AW	
56009/56201		LB		56094	COLO	RU	
56018	NRHL	AW		56096	EPEX	AW	
56032		HQ	stored Kingsbury	56098	NRHL	HQ	at Shackerstone
56037		HQ	stored Shackerstone	56103	HTLX	AW	
56038		BO		56105	COLO	RU	
56051	COLS	AW		56113	COLS	AW	
56060	NRHL	AW		56117	EPEX	BO	
56065	NRHL	BO		56128	HTLX	AW	at Wansford
56077		HQ	stored Shackerstone	56301	HTLX	BO	
56078	COLS	AW		56302	COLO	RU	
56081	NRHL	BO		56303	HTLX	AW	Brian
56086	EPEX	AW		56311	HTLX	AW	
56087	COLO	RU		56312	HTLX	AW	

56301/302/303/311/312 re-numbered from 56045/124/125/057/003.

CLASS 57 TYPE 5 Co-Co

Rebuilt: 1998-2000 from Cl 47 at Loughborough **Maximum Speed:** 75 mph
Weight: 121 tonnes **Engine:** General Motors 645 V12 2500 hp
Route Availability: 6 **Transmission:** Brush Traction Motors
Maximum Tractive Effort: 55,000 lbf **Wheel Diameter:** 1143 mm

57001 (47356)	AWCA	CS	57007 (47332)	XHCK	KM
57002 (47322)	XHSS	ZG	57008 (47060)	XHCK	KM
57003 (47317)	XHCK	KM	57009 (47079)	XHCK	KM
57004 (47347)	XHCK	KM	57010 (47231)	XHCK	KM
57005 (47350)	AWCX	CS	57011 (47329)	XHCK	KM
57006 (47187)	AWCA	CS	57012 (47204)	XHSS	ZA

57008 Telford International Railfreight Park June - 2009

57/3 Fitted Electric Train heat Rebuilt: 2002 onwards from Cl 47 at Loughborough

Engine: General Motors 654F3B 2750 hp
Fitted with Dellner coupling *removed

Maximum Speed: 95 mph
Weight: 117 tonnes

57301 (47845)	QADD	HQ	
57302 (47827)	XHAC	KM	Chad Varah
57303 (47705)	QADD	ZG	
57304 (47807)	XHAC	KM	Pride of Cheshire
57305 (47822)	QADD	HQ	
57306 (47814)	QADD	HQ	
57307 (47225)	XHAC	KM	LADY PENELOPE
57308 (47846)	XHAC	KM	
57309 (47806)	XHAC	KM	Pride of Crewe
57310 (47831)	QADD	HQ	
57311 (47817)	XHAC	KM	
57312 (47330)	QADD	HQ	Peter Henderson
57313 (47371)*	AWCX	BH	
57314 (47372)*	AWCX	BH	
57315 (47234)*	AWCX	BH	
57316 (47290)*	AWCX	BH	

57/6 Fitted Electric Train heat
Rebuilt: 2001/*03 onwards from Cl 47 at Loughborough.

Maximum Speed: 95 mph
Weight: 113 tonnes

57601 (47825)	AWCA	CS	*Sheila*
57602* (47337)	EFOO	OO	Restormel Castle
57603* (47349)	EFOO	OO	Tintagel Castle
57604* (47209)	EFOO	OO	PENDENNIS CASTLE
57605* (47206)	EFOO	OO	Totnes Castle

CLASS 58 B.R.E.L. TYPE 5 Co-Co

Built: 1983-7
Weight: 130 tonnes
Maximum Tractive Effort: 61,800 lbf
Transmission: Six Brush Traction Motors

Maximum Speed: 80 mph
Engine: Rushton-Paxman 3300 hp
Wheel Diameter: 1120 mm
Route Availability: 7

58001	WNTS	Amiens, France
58002	WNSO	EH
58004	WNTS	AZ
58005	WNTS	France
58006	WNTS	AZ
58007	WNTS	France
58008	WNTS	EH (grounded)
58009	WNTS	France
58010	WNTS	France
58011	WNTS	AZ

58012	WNTS	TT	58035	WNTS	France
58013	WNTS	Amiens, France	58036	WNTS	France
58017	WNXX	EH	58037	WNXX	EH
58018	WNTS	France	58038	WNTS	Amiens, France
58021	WNTS	France	58039	WNTS	France
58022	WNTS	CD	58040	WNTS	AZ
58023	WNTS	TT	58042	WNTS	AZ
58025	WNTS	Albacete, Spain	58044	WZFF	France
58026	WNTS	AZ	58046	WNTS	France
58027	WNTS	Albacete, Spain	58048	WNTS	CE
58032	WNTS	France	58049	WNTS	AZ
58033	WNTS	France	58050	WNTS	Albacete, Spain
58034	WNTS	Amiens, France			

58015/020/024/029/030/031/041/043/047 - sold to Transfesa Group, Spain and de-registered

CLASS 59 GENERAL MOTORS TYPE 5 Co-Co

Engine: General Motors 3300 hp **Maximum Speed:** 60 mph
Weight: 121 tonnes **Wheel Diameter:** 1067 mm
Maximum Tractive Effort: 113,550 lbf **Route Availability:** 7
Transmission: General Motors D77B Traction Motors

59/0 Owned by Holeim Aggregate Industries. Built: 1985/*9 in USA/*Illinois

59001	XYPO	MD	YEOMAN ENDEAVOUR	59004	XYPO	MD	PAUL A HAMMOND
59002	XYPO	MD	ALAN J DAY	59005·	XYPO	MD	KENNETH J. PAINTER

59/1 Owned by Hanson Quarry Products. Built: 1990 in Canada

59101	XYPA	MD	Village of Whatley	59103	XYPA	MD	Village of Mells
59102	XYPA	MD	Village of Chantry	59104	XYPA	MD	Village of Great Elm

59/2 Owned by D B Schenker

Built: 59201 in 1993, 59202-59206 in 1995 at London, Ontario, Canada
Maximum Speed: 75 mph

59201	WDAK	TO	59204	WDAK	TO	
59202	WFMU	TO	59205	WDAK	TO	
59203	WDAK	TO	59206	WDAK	TO	John F. Yeoman Rail Pioneer

CLASS 60 BRUSH TYPE 5 Co-Co

Built: 1989-1992
Weight: 129-131 tonnes
Maximum Tractive Effort: 106,500 lbf
Transmission: Brush Traction Motors

Maximum Speed: 60 mph
Engine: Mirrlees 3,100 hp
Wheel Diameter: 1118 mm
Route Availability: 7

60001	WNWX	TO	The Railway Observer
60002	WNTS	CD	High Peak
60003	WNTS	TO	FREIGHT TRANSPORT ASSOCIATION
60004	WNTS	Toton Yard	
60005	WNTS	Toton Yard	
60006	WNTS	Toton Yard	
60007	WCBI	TO	The Spirit of Tom Kendell
60008	WNTS	TT	Sir William McAlpine
60009	WNTS	TO	
60010	WCBI	TO	
60011	WCAI	TO	
60012	WNWX	TO	
60013	WNTR	TT	Robert Boyle
60014	WNTS	Toton Yard	
60015	WCBI	TO	
60017	WCBK	TO	
60018	WNTS	Toton Yard	
60019	WCAK	TO	Port of Grimsby & Immingham
60020	WCBI	TO	
60021	WNTS	TO	
60022	WNTS	TO	
60023	WNTS	Toton Yard	
60024	WNWX	TO	
60025	WNTS	Toton Yard	
60026	WNTS	TT	
60027	WNTS	Toton Yard	
60028	WNTS	CD	John Flamsteed
60029	WNTS	CD	Clitheroe Castle
60030	WNTS	TO	
60031	WNTS	Toton Yard	
60032	WNTS	Toton Yard	
60033	WNWX	TO	Tees Steel Express
60034	WNTS	TT	Carnedd Llewelyn (one side only)
60035	WNTR	TO	
60036	WNTS	TT	GEFCO
60037	WNTS	Toton Yard	
60038	WNTS	CD	AvestaPolarit
60039	WNTR	TO	
60040	WCAI	TO	The Territorial Army Centenary
60041	WNTS	TO	

60042	WNTS	Toton Yard	
60043	WNTS	TO	
60044	WNWX	BZ	
60045	WCAI	TO	The Permanent Way Institution
60046	WNTS	CD	William Wilberforce (one side only)
60047	WNTS	CD	
60048	WNTS	TO	
60049	WSSK	OX	
60050	WNTS	Toton Yard	
60051	WNTS	TO	
60052	WNTS	TO	Glofa Tŵr/Tower Colliery The last deep mine in Wales
60053	WNTS	Toton Yard	
60054	WCBI	TO	
60055	WNTS	CD	Thomas Barnado
60056	WNTS	CD	William Beveridge
60057	WNTS	TT	Adam Smith
60058	WNTS	TO	
60059	WCBK	TO	Swinden Dalesman
60060	WNTS	Toton Yard	
60061	WNTS	TO (spares)	
60062	WNWX	TO	
60063	WCAI	TO	
60064	WNTS	TO	Back Tor (one side only)
60065	WFMU	TO	Spirit of Jaguar
60066	WNWX	TO	John Logie Baird (one side only)
60067	WNTS	Toton Yard	
60068	WNTS	TO	
60069	WNTS	TO	Slioch
60070	WNTS	TO	
60071	WCBK	EH	Ribblehead Viaduct
60072	WNTS	TT	Cairn Toul (one side only)
60073	WNTS	TO	Cairn Gorm (one side only)
60074	WCAI	TO	Teenage Spirit
60075	WNTS	TO	
60076	WNTS	CD	
60077	WNTS	TT	
60078	WNTS	Toton Yard	
60079	WCAI	TO	
60080	WNTS	TO	
60081	WNTS	Toton Yard	
60082	WNTS	CD	
60083	WNTS	Toton Yard	
60084	WNTS	TT	
60085	WNTS	TT	MINI - Pride of Oxford
60086	WNTS	Toton Yard	
60087	WNWX	TO	
60088	WNTS	Toton Yard	

60089	WNTS	Toton Yard	
60090	WNTS	TT	Quinag (one side only)
60091	WFMU	TO	
60092	WCBI	TO	
60093	WNTS	Toton Yard	
60094	WNTS	TT	Rugby Flyer
60095	WNTS	CD	
60096	WNTS	BZ	
60097	WNTS	Toton Yard	
60098	WNTS	TT	
60099	WCAI	TO	
60100	WNWX	BZ	
60500(60016)	WNTS	TT	

CLASS 66 GENERAL MOTORS TYPE 5 Co - Co

Built: 1998 - 2008 in Ontario, Canada
Maximum Speed: 75 mph
Weight:126 tonnes
Engine: GM 710 3,200 hp
Route Availability: 7
Wheel Diameter: 1066mm
Maximum Tractive Effort: 92,000 lbf
knuckle autocoupler fitted
Transmission: General Motors, D43 Traction Motors

66001	WBAI	TO	
66002	WBAL	TO	Lafarge Quorn
66003	WBAI	TO	
66004	WBAI	TO	
66005	WBAK	TO	
66006	WNWX	TO	
66007	WBAI	TO	
66008	WSSI	TO	
66009	WBAK	TO	
66010	WBEN	AZ	
66011	WBAK	TO	
66012	WBAI	TO	
66013	WBAL	TO	
66014	WBAK	TO	
66015	WBAK	TO	
66016	WBAI	TO	
66017	WBAK	TO	
66018	WBAK	TO	
66019	WBAL	TO	
66020	WBAI	TO	
66021	WBAI	TO	
66022	WBEN	AZ	
66023	WBAI	TO	
66024	WBAK	TO	
66025	WBAL	TO	
66026	WBEN	AZ	
66027	WBAK	TO	
66028	WBEN	AZ	
66029	WBEN	AZ	
66030	WBAI	TO	
66031	WBAK	TO	
66032	WBEN	AZ	
66033	WBEN	AZ	
66034	WBAK	TO	
66035	WBAI	TO	
66036	WBEN	AZ	
66037	WBAK	TO	
66038	WBEN	AZ	
66039	WBAI	TO	
66040	WBAK	TO	

66041	WBAI	TO	
66042	WBEN	AZ	
66043	WBAK	TO	
66044	WBAI	TO	
66045	WBEN	AZ	TO
66046	WBAI	TO	
66047	WBAL	TO	
66048	WNTS	TO	James the Engine
66049	WBEN	AZ	
66050	WBAK	TO	EWS Energy
66051	WFMU	TO	
66052	WBEN	AZ	
66053	WBAK	TO	
66054	WBAL	TO	
66055	WFMU	TO	
66056	WBLI	TO	
66057	WBLI	TO	
66058	WBAL	TO	
66059	WBAK	TO	
66060	WBAK	TO	
66061	WFMU	TO	
66062	WBEN	AZ	
66063	WBAK	TO	
66064	WBEN	AZ	
66065	WBAI	TO	
66066	WBAL	TO	
66067	WBAK	TO	
66068	WBAI	TO	
66069	WBAK	TO	
66070	WBAK	TO	
66071	WBEN	AZ	
66072	WBEN	AZ	
66073	WBEN	AZ	
66074	WBAL	TO	
66075	WBAI	TO	
66076	WBAI	TO	
66077	WBAK	TO	Benjamin Gimbert GC
66078	WBAI	TO	
66079	WBAL	TO	James Nightall GC
66080	WNTR	TO	
66081	WBAK	TO	
66082	WBAL	TO	
66083	WBAI	TO	
66084	WBAI	TO	
66085	WBAI	TO	

66086	WBAK	TO
66087	WBAI	TO
66088	WBAK	TO
66089	WBAI	TO
66090	WBAL	TO
66091	WBAK	TO
66092	WBAK	TO
66093	WBAL	TO
66094	WBAL	TO
66095	WBAL	TO
66096	WBAK	TO
66097	WBAK	TO
66098	WBAK	TO
66099	WBBK	TO
66100	WBBI	TO
66101	WBAI	TO
66102	WBBI	TO
66103	WBBK	TO
66104	WBBI	TO
66105	WBBI	TO
66106	WBBI	TO
66107	WBBI	TO
66108	WBBL	TO
66109	WBAI	TO
66110	WBBI	TO
66111	WBBL	TO
66112	WBBI	TO
66113	WBBK	TO
66114	WBBI	TO
66115	WBAI	TO
66116	WBAI	TO
66117	WBAK	TO
66118	WFMU	TO
66119	WBAK	TO
66120	WBAK	TO
66121	WBAK	TO
66122	WBAL	TO
66123	WBEN	AZ
66124	WBAL	TO
66125	WBAK	TO
66126	WBAK	TO
66127	WBAL	TO
66128	WBAI	TO
66129	WBAK	TO
66130	WBAI	TO

66131	WFMU	TO	
66132	WSSK	DR	
66133	WBAK	TO	
66134	WBAL	TO	
66135	WBAI	TO	
66136	WBAI	TO	
66137	WBAL	TO	
66138	WBAK	TO	
66139	WBAK	TO	
66140	WBAK	TO	
66141	WBAK	TO	
66142	WBAK	TO	
66143	WBAL	TO	
66144	WBAI	TO	
66145	WBAI	TO	
66146	WBEP	PN	
66147	WBAI	TO	
66148	WBAK	TO	
66149	WBAI	TO	
66150	WBAK	TO	
66151	WSSK	TO	
66152	WBAK	TO	Derek Holmes Railway Operator
66153	WBEP	PN	
66154	WBAI	TO	
66155	WBAI	TO	
66156	WBAI	TO	
66157	WBEP	PN	
66158	WBAK	TO	
66159	WBEP	PN	
66160	WBAI	TO	
66161	WBAI	TO	
66162	WBAI	TO	
66163	WBEP	PN	
66164	WBAL	TO	
66165	WBAI	TO	
66166	WBEP	PN	
66167	WBAK	TO	
66168	WBAI	TO	
66169	WBAL	TO	
66170	WBAK	TO	
66171	WBAK	TO	
66172	WBAK	TO	Paul Meleny
66173	WBEP	PN	
66174	WBAI	TO	
66175	WBAI	TO	
66176	WBAK	TO	
66177	WBAI	TO	
66178	WBEP	PN	
66179	WBEN	AZ	
66180	WBEP	PN	
66181	WBAI	TO	18/5/10
66182	WBAI	TO	
66183	WBAK	TO	
66184	WBAI	TO	
66185	WBAL	TO	
66186	WBAI	TO	
66187	WBAI	TO	
66188	WBAI	TO	
66189	WBEP	PN	
66190	WBEN	AZ	
66191	WBEN	AZ	
66192	WBAI	TO	
66193	WFMU	TO	
66194	WBAL	TO	
66195	WBEN	AZ	
66196	WBEP	PN	
66197	WBAI	TO	
66198	WBAK	TO	
66199	WBAI	TO	
66200	WBAK	TO	RAILWAY HERITAGE COMMITTEE
66201	WBAI	TO	
66202	WBEN	AZ	
66203	WBEN	AZ	
66204	WBAI	TO	
66205	WBEN	AZ	
66206	WBAI	TO	
66207	WBAL	TO	
66208	WBEN	AZ	
66209	WBEN	AZ	
66210	WBEN	AZ	
66211	WBEN	AZ	
66212	WBEN	AZ	
66213	WBAK	TO	
66214	WBEN	AZ	
66215	WBEN	AZ	
66216	WBEN	AZ	
66217	WBEN	AZ	
66218	WBEN	AZ	

66219	WBEN	AZ
66220	WBEP	PN
66221	WBAI	TO
66222	WBEN	AZ
66223	WBEN	AZ
66224	WBEN	AZ
66225	WBEN	AZ
66226	WBEN	AZ
66227	WBEP	PN
66228	WBEN	AZ
66229	WBEN	AZ
66230	WBAI	TO
66231	WBEN	AZ
66232	WBAK	TO
66233	WBEN	AZ
66234	WBEN	AZ
66235	WBEN	AZ
66236	WBEN	AZ
66237	WBEP	PN
66238	WBAL	TO
66239	WBEN	AZ
66240	WBEN	AZ
66241	WBEN	AZ
66242	WBEN	AZ
66243	WBEN	AZ
66244	WBEN	AZ
66245	WBEN	AZ
66246	WBEN	AZ
66247	WBEN	AZ
66248	WBEP	PN
66249	WBEN	AZ
66250	WBAK	TO

66250 carries inscription on cab side:
In Memory of Robert K. Romak

66/3 Low emission (3245hp)

66301	XHIM	KM
66302	XHIM	KM
66303	XHIM	KM
66304	XHIM	KM
66305	XHIM	KM

66/4

66411	DFEP	Poland
66412	DFEP	Poland
66413	DFHG	FD
66414	DFIN	FD
66415	DFTZ	FD
66416	DFIN	FD
66417	DFEP	Poland
66418	DFIN	FD
66419	DFTZ	FD
66420	DFIN	FD
66421	XHIM	KM
66422	XHIM	KM
66423	XHIM	KM
66424	XHIM	KM
66425	XHIM	KM
66426	XHIM	KM
66427	XHIM	KM
66428	XHIM	KM
66429	XHIM	KM
66430	XHIM	KM
66431	XHIM	KM
66432	XHIM	KM
66433	XHIM	KM
66434	XHIM	KM

66/5

66501	DFGM	FD	Japan 2001
66502	DFGM	FD	Basford Hall Centenary 2001
66503	DFGM	FD	The RAILWAY MAGAZINE
66504	DFGM	FD	
66505	DFGM	FD	
66506	DFHH	FD	Crewe Regeneration
66507	DFHH	FD	
66508	DFRT	FD	
66509	DFHH	FD	
66510	DFRT	FD	
66511	DFRT	FD	
66512	DFHH	FD	
66513	DFHH	FD	
66514	DFRT	FD	
66515	DFRT	FD	
66516	DFGM	FD	
66517	DFGM	FD	
66518	DFHH	FD	
66519	DFHH	FD	
66520	DFRT	FD	
66522	DFRT	LD	east london express
66523	DFRT	FD	
66524	DFHH	LD	
66525	DFHH	FD	
66526	DFHH	LD	Driver Steve Dunn (George)
66527	DFRT	LD	Don Raider
66528	DFHH	FD	
66529	DFHH	FD	
66530	DFHH	LD	
66531	DFHH	FD	
66532	DFGM	FD	P&O Nedlloyd Atlas
66533	DFGM	FD	Hanjin Express/ Senator Express
66534	DFGM	FD	OOCL EXPRESS
66535	DFHH	FD	
66536	DFHH	FD	
66537	DFGM	FD	
66538	DFIM	FD	
66539	DFHG	FD	
66540	DFIM	FD	Ruby
66541	DFIM	FD	
66542	DFIM	FD	
66543	DFIM	FD	
66544	DFHG	LD	
66545	DFHG	FD	
66546	DFHG	FD	
66547	DFHG	LD	
66548	DFHG	LD	
66549	DFHG	LD	
66550	DFHG	FD	
66551	DFHG	LD	
66552	DFHG	LD	Maltby Raider
66553	DFHG	LD	
66554	DFHG	LD	
66555	DFHG	LD	
66556	DFIM	LD	
66557	DFHG	FD	
66558	DFIM	FD	
66559	DFHG	LD	
66560	DFHG	FD	
66561	DFHG	FD	
66562	DFIM	LD	
66563	DFIM	FD	
66564	DFIM	LD	
66565	DFIM	LD	
66566	DFIM	LD	
66567	DFIM	FD	
66568	DFIM	FD	
66569	DFIM	FD	
66570	DFIM	FD	
66571	DFIM	FD	
66572	DFIM	FD	
66582	DHLT	Poland	
66583	DHLT	Poland	
66584	DHLT	Poland	
66585	DFHG	FD	The Drax Flyer
66586	DHLT	Poland	
66587	DFIN	FD	
66588	DFIN	FD	
66589	DFIN	FD	
66590	DFIN	FD	
66591	DFIN	FD	
66592	DFIN	FD	Johnson Stevens Agencies

66593	DFIN	FD	3MG MERSEY MULTIMODAL GATEWAY
66594	DFIN	FD	NYK Spirit of Kyoto
66595	DFHG	FD	
66596	DFHG	FD	
66597	DFHG	FD	Viridor
66598	DFHG	FD	
66599	DFHG	FD	

66582/583/584/586 carry numbers 66-009/010/011/008

66/6 Fitted with modified gear ratios. Max. Speed: 65 mph. Max. TE: 105,080 lbf

66601	DFHH	FD	The Hope Valley
66602	DFHH	FD	
66603	DFHH	FD	
66604	DFHH	FD	
66605	DFHH	FD	
66606	DFHH	FD	
66607	DFHG	FD	
66608	DFEP	Poland	
66609	DFEP	Poland	
66610	DFHG	FD	
66611	DFEP	Poland	
66612	DFEP	Poland	Forth Raider
66613	DFHG	FD	
66614	DFHG	FD	
66615	DFHG	FD	
66616	DFHG	FD	
66617	DFHG	FD	
66618	DFHG	FD	Railways Illustrated Annual Photographic Awards Alan Barnes
66619	DFHG	FD	Derek W. Johnson MB
66620	DFHG	FD	
66621	DFHG	FD	
66622	DFHG	FD	
66623	DFHG	FD	Bill Bolsover
66624	DHLT	Poland	carries number 66-10
66625	DHLT	Poland	carries number 66-10

66/7 Operated by GB Railfreight

(66733-737 renumbered from 66401-405) (66738-741 renumbered from 66578-66581)

66701	GBCM	PG	
66702	GBCM	PG	Blue Lightning
66703	GBCM	SV	Doncaster PSB 1981-2002
66704	GBCM	SV	Colchester Power Signalbox
66705	GBCM	SV	Golden Jubilee
66706	GBCM	SV	Nene Valley
66707	GBCM	SV	Sir Sam Fay GREAT CENTRAL RAILWAY
66708	GBCM	PG	Jayne
66709	GBCM	PG	Sorrento
66710	GBCM	SV	Phil Packer BRIT
66711	GBCM	SV	
66712	GBCM	SV	Peterborough Power Signalbox
66713	GBCM	SV	Forest City
66714	GBCM	SV	Cromer Lifeboat
66715	GBCM	SV	VALOUR IN MEMORY OF ALL RAILWAY EMPLOYEES WHO GAVE THEIR LIVES FOR THEIR COUNTRY
66716	GBCM	SV	LOCOMOTIVE & CARRIAGE INSTITUTION CENTENARY 1911-201
66717	GBCM	SV	Good Old Boy
66718	GBCM	SV	Gwyneth Dunwoody
66719	GBCM	SV	METRO-LAND
66720	GBCM	SV	
66721	GBCM	SV	Harry Beck
66722	GBCM	SV	Sir Edward Watkin
66723	GBSD	PG	Chinook
66724	GBSD	PG	Drax Power Station
66725	GBSD	PG	SUNDERLAND
66726	GBSD	PG	SHEFFIELD WEDNESDAY
66727	GBSD	PG	Andrew Scott CBE

66728	GBCM	PG	Institution of Railway Operators	66739	GBCM	PG	
66729	GBCM	PG	DERBY COUNTY	66740	GBCM	PG	
66730	GBCM	PG	Whitemoor	66741	GBCM	PG	
66731	GBCM	PG	interhubGB	66742	GBRT	PG	ABP Port of Immingham Centenary 1912-2012
66732	GBCM	PG	GBRf The First Decade 1999 – 2009 John Smith - MD	66743	GBRT	PG	
66733	GBFM	PG		66744	GBRT	PG	Crossrail
66734	SBXL	HQ	(accident at Loch Treig)	66745	GBRT	PG	Modern Railways The First 50 Years
66735	GBFM	PG		66746	GBRT	PG	
66736	GBFM	PG	WOLVERHAMPTON WANDERERS	66747	GBNL	HQ	SK
66737	GBFM	PG	Lesia	66748	GBNL	HQ	SK
66738	GBCM	PG		66749	GBNL	HQ	SK

66/8 (66841-845 overhauled and renumbered from 66406-410 then renumbered 66742-746)
66846-850 renumbered from 66573-577

66846	COLO	RU		66849	COLO	RU	Wylam Dilly
66847	COLO	RU		66850	COLO	RU	
66848	COLO	RU					

66/9 Low Emission   Max. TE: 105,080 lbf

66951	DFHG	FD	66955	DFIN	FD
66952	DFHG	FD	66956	DFHG	FD
66953	DFHG	FD	66957	DFHG	FD
66954	DFIN	FD	Stephenson Locomotive Society 1909-2009		

CLASS 67   GENERAL MOTORS   TYPE 5   Bo - Bo

Built: 1999 - 2000 in Spain under contract to GM
Weight: 90 tonnes
Route Availability: 8
Maximum Tractive Effort: 31,770 lbf
Transmission: General Motors, D43 Traction Motors
Maximum Speed: 125 mph
Engine: GM 710 3,200 hp
Wheel Diameter: 965mm

67001	WATN	CE		67005	WAAN	CE	Queen's Messenger
67002	WATN	CE		67006	WAAN	CE	Royal Sovereign
67003	WFMU	TO		67007	WAAN	CE	
67004	WABN	CE	Post haste	67008	WAAN	CE	

67009	WFMU	CE		67020	WAAN	CE	
67010	WAWN	CE		67021	WAAN	CE	
67011	WNWX	CE		67022	WAAN	CE	
67012	WAWN	CE	A Shropshire Lad	67023	WAAN	CE	
67013	WAWN	CE	Dyfrbont Pontcysyllte	67024	WAAN	CE	
67014	WAWN	CE	Thomas Telford	67025	WFMU	CE	Western Star
67015	WAWN	CE	David J. Lloyd	67026	WAAN	CE	Diamond Jubilee
67016	WFMU	CE		67027	WAAN	CE	Rising Star
67017	WNTR	CE	Arrow	67028	WAAN	TO	
67018	WFMU	CE	Keith Heller	67029	WATN	CE	Royal Diamond
67019	WAAN	CE		67030	WABN	CE	

67004/027 name on one side only

CLASS 68 VOSSLOH UKLIGHT TYPE 5 Bo - Bo

Built: 2013 in Valencia, Spain due from late 2013
Weight: 85 tonnes
Route Availability:
Maximum Tractive Effort: 71,265 lbf
Transmission: 4 ABB AC Traction Motors

Maximum Speed: 100 mph
Engine: Caterpillar c175, 3,750 hp
Wheel Diameter: 1100mm

68001
68002
68003
68004
68005
68006
68007
68008
68009
68010
68011
68012
68013
68014
68015

On order for DRS

CLASS 70 GENERAL ELECTRIC TYPE 5 Co - Co

Built: November 2009 onwards **Maximum Speed:** 75 mph
Weight: 129 tonnes **Engine:** GEJP 616 3,700 hp
Route Availability: 7 **Wheel Diameter:** 1067mm
Maximum Tractive Effort: 120,000 lbf
Transmission: General Electric, acTraction Motors

70001	DFGI	FD	PowerHaul
70002	DFGH	FD	
70003	DFGH	FD	
70004	DFGH	FD	The Coal Industry Society
70005	DFGH	FD	
70006	DFGH	FD	
70007	DFGI	FD	
70008	DFGI	FD	
70009	DFGI	FD	
70010	DFGH	FD	
70011	DFGH	FD	
70013	DFGH	FD	
70014	DFGH	FD	
70015	DFGH	FD	
70016	DFGH	FD	
70017	DFGI	FD	
70018	DFGI	FD	
70019	DFGI	FD	
70020	DFGI	FD	
70021			
70022			
70023			
70024			
70025			
70026			
70027			
70028			
70029			
70030			
70099	MBDL	LB	

70012 was damaged and returned to USA

CLASS 73 BR/ENGLISH ELECTRIC ELECTRO-DIESEL Bo-Bo

Built: 1962-7 **Maximum Speed:** 60-90 mph
Weight: 76-77 tonnes **Maximum Tractive Effort:** 34,000 - 42,000 lbf
Engine: English Electric 600 hp/*Cummins 1500 hp
Voltage: 660-750 V DC Third Rail **Wheel Diameter:** 1016mm
Transmission: Four English Electric Traction Motors **Route Availability:** 6

73/1

73101	RVLS	ZA	
73103	NRLS	HQ	(stored at Throckmorton)
73104*	RVLS	ZA	
73105	NRLS	HQ	(stored at Shackerstone)
73107	MBED	SE	Redhill 1844-1994

73109	MBED	SL	Battle of Britain 50th Anniversary
73114	NRLO	HQ	at Battlefield Railway, Shackerstone
73117	NRLS	BO	
73118	MBED	Barry (s)	
73119	GBED	SE	Borough of Eastleigh
73133	MBED	Barry	
73134	NRLS	BO	
73136	MBED	SL	Perseverance
73138	QADD	ZA	
73139	RVLO	ZAs	
73141	GBED	SE	Charlotte

73/2 Air brake only. Gatwick Express X MTU 1600 hp engine

73201	MBED	SE	Broadlands
73202	MBED	SL	Dave Berry
73204	GBED	SE	Janice
73205	GBED	SE	Jeanette
73206	GBED	SE	Lisa
73207	GBED	SE	
73208	GBED	SE	Kirsten
73209x	GBZZ	LB	Alison
73211*	MBED	ZAs	
73212	GBED	SE	
73213	GBED	SE	
73235	HYWD	BM	

These AC Electric Locos are preserved

81002	E3003	ACXX	BH
82008	E3054	ACXX	BH
83012	E3035	ACXX	BH
84001x	E3036	ACXX	BH
85101	E3061	ACXX	BH
86213	Lancashire Witch	ACXX	WB
86401	86001 Northampton Town	ACAC	WN
89001		ACXX	BH

x owned by the National Railway Museum

CLASS 86 BRITISH RAIL/ENGLISH ELECTRIC Bo-Bo

86/1 modified at Crewe with 87/0 motors and bogies.

Built: Vulcan Foundry 1965
Weight: 87 tonnes
Maximum Tractive Effort: 58,000 lbf
Transmission: Four GEC Traction Motors
Maximum Speed: 110 mph
Voltage: 25 kV AC Overhead
Wheel Diameter: 1150mm
Route Availability: 6

86101	ETLO	CP	Sir William A Stanier

86/2 modified at Crewe from 86/0 with flexicoil springs and SAB resilient wheels.

vacuum brake isolated/removed.

Built: 1965-66
Weight: 83-87 tonnes
Maximum Tractive Effort: 46,500 lbf
Transmission: Four AEI Traction Motors

Maximum Speed: 100 mph
Voltage: 25 kV AC Overhead
Wheel Diameter: 1156mm
Route Availability: 6

86228#	EPEX	LM	86235#	EPUK	LM	86247#	DHLT	CP
86229#	EPEX	LM	86242#	EPUK	LM	86251#	EPEX	LM
86231#	EPUK	LM	86246#	EPEX	LM	86259#	MBEL	WN
86234#	EPEX	LM						

86259 also carries number E3137 and named Les Ross.

86/4 modified at Crewe from 86/0 and 86/3 fitted with flexicoil springs and resilient wheels

vacuum brake isolated/removed

86424#	ETLS	LM

86/6 designated for Freight Sector use (restricted to 75 mph Max.)

86501(608)	DFGC	FE	86613	DFNC	FE	86632	DFNC	FE
86604	DFNC	FE	86614	DFNC	FE	86633	EPXX	CP
86605	DFNC	FE	86621	EPXX	CP	86635	EPXX	CP
86607	DFNC	FE	86622	DFNC	FE	86637	DFNC	FE
86609	DFNC	FE	86627	DFNC	FE	86638	DFNC	FE
86610	DFNC	FE	86628	DFNC	FE	86639	DFNC	FE
86612	DFNC	FE						

All air brake only. 86633/35 are grounded

86/7 Constellation AC Electrics (110 mph)

86701(205)	EPUK	WNs	Orion
86702(260)	EPUK	IL	Cassiopeia

86/9 Mobile Load Bank (restricted to 60 mph Max.)

86901(253)	QACL	ZA	CHIEF ENGINEER
86902(210)	QACL	ZA	RAIL VEHICLE ENGINEERING

CLASS 87 BRITISH RAIL Bo-Bo

Built: 1973-75
Weight: 83.5 tonnes
Maximum Tractive Effort: 58,000 lbf
Transmission: Four GEC Traction Motors
Maximum Speed: 110 mph
Voltage: 25 kV AC Overhead
Wheel Diameter: 1150mm
Route Availability: 6

87/0

87001	MBEL	YK	87002	ETLO	WN

87001 Royal Scot/STEPHENSON. 87002 Royal Sovereign.

CLASS 90 B.R.E.L./GENERAL ELECTRIC CO Bo-Bo

Built: 1987-90
Weight: 84.5 tonnes
Route Availability: 6
Maximum Tractive Effort: 43,100 lbf
Transmission: GEC Traction Motors
Maximum Speed: 110 mph
Voltage: 25 kV AC Overhead
Wheel Diameter: 1156mm

90001	IANA	NC	
90002	IANA	NC	
90003	IANA	NC	Rædwald of East Anglia
90004	IANA	NC	Eastern Daily Press, 1870 -2010, SERVING NORFOLK FOR 140 YEARS
90005	IANA	NC	Vice-Admiral Lord Nelson
90006	IANA	NC	Modern Railways Magazine/Roger Ford
90007	IANA	NC	Sir John Betjeman
90008	IANA	NC	The East Anglian
90009	IANA	NC	
90010	IANA	NC	BRESSINGHAM STEAM & GARDENS
90011	IANA	NC	Let's Go East of England
90012	IANA	NC	Royal Anglian Regiment
90013	IANA	NC	The Evening Star PRIDE OF IPSWICH 1885-2010 125 YEARS OF SERVING SUFFOLK
90014	IANA	NC	Norfolk and Norwich Festival
90015	IANA	NC	Colchester Castle
90016	DFLC	FE	
90017	WNTS	CE	
90018	WEFE	CE	
90019	WEFE	CE	

90020	WEFE	CE	Collingwood
90021	WEFE	CE	
90022	WNTS	CE	Freight**connection**
90023	WNTS	CE	
90024	WNTR	CE	
90025	WNTS	CE	
90026	WEFE	CE	
90027	WNTS	CE	Allerton T&RS Depot - Quality Approved
90028	WNTR	CE	
90029	WEFE	CE	
90030	WNTS	CE	Crewe Locomotive Works
90031	WNTS	CE	The Railway Children Partnership Working for Street Children Worldwide
90032	WNTS	CE	
90033	WNTS	CE	
90034	WNTS	CE	
90035	WNTR	CE	
90036	WEFE	CE	
90037	WNTS	CE	Spirit of Dagenham
90038	WNTS	CE	
90039	WEFE	CE	
90040	WNTS	CE	The Railway Mission
90041	DFLC	FE	
90042	DFLC	FE	
90043	DFLC	FE	Freightliner Coatbridge
90044	DFLC	FE	
90045	DFLC	FE	
90046	DFLC	FE	
90047	DFLC	FE	
90048	DFLC	FE	
90049	DFLC	FE	
90050	MBEL	CP	

CLASS 91 B.R.E.L./GENERAL ELECTRIC CO Bo-Bo

Built: 1988-91
Weight: 84 tonnes
Route Availability: 7
Maximum Tractive Effort: 42,700 lbf
Transmission: GEC Traction Motors
Maximum Speed: 140 mph
Voltage: 25 kV AC Overhead
Wheel Diameter: 1000mm

91/1 (Refurbished and renumbered from 910xx) 91132 renumbered from 91023.
*91107 carries No. 91007.

91101	IECA	BN	91112	IECA	BN	91122	IECA	BN
91102	IECA	BN	91113	IECA	BN	91124	IECA	BN
91103	IECA	BN	91114	IECA	BN	91125	IECA	BN
91104	IECA	BN	91115	IECA	BN	91126	IECA	BN
91105	IECA	BN	91116	IECA	BN	91127	IECA	BN
91106	IECA	BN	91117	IECA	BN	91128	IECA	BN
91107*	IECA	BN	91118	IECA	BN	91129	IECA	BN
91108	IECA	BN	91119	IECA	BN	91130	IECA	BN
91109	IECA	BN	91120	IECA	BN	91131	IECA	BN
91110	IECA	BN	91121	IECA	BN	91132	IECA	BN
91111	IECA	BN						

91102 City of York. 91007 SKYFALL. 91109 Sir Bobby Robson.
91110 Battle of Britain MEMORIAL FLIGHT SPITFIRE, HURRICANE, LANCASTER, DAKOTA.
91115 Blaydon Races. 91117 WEST RIDING LIMITED.

CLASS 92 BRUSH Co - Co

Built: 1993-1995
Weight: 126 tonnes
Dual Voltage: 25 kV AC Overhead/750v DC third rail
Maximum Tractive Effort: 89,920 lbf
Transmission: Brush Traction Motors
Maximum Speed: 100 mph
Route Availability: 7
Wheel Diameter: 1160 mm

92001	WNTR	CE	Victor Hugo
92002	WTAE	CE	H.G. Wells
92003	WFMU	CE	Beethoven
92004	WNWX	CE	Jane Austen
92005	WNTR	CE	Mozart

92006	PTXX	CO	Louis Armand
92007	WNTR	CE	Schubert
92008	WNWX	CE	Jules Verne
92009	WNTR	CE	Marco Polo
92010	PTXX	CO	Molière
92011	WTAE	CE	Handel
92012	WNTR	CE	Thomas Hardy
92013	WNWX	CE	Puccini
92014	PTXX	CO	Emile Zola
92015	WTHE	CE	
92016	WTHE	CE	
92017	WNTR	CE	Bart the Engine
92018	PTXX	CO	Stendhal
92019	WTAE	CE	Wagner
92020	PTXX	CO	Milton
92021	PTXX	CO	Purcell
92022	WNTR	CE	Charles Dickens
92023	PTXX	CO	Ravel
92024	WNWX	CE	J S Bach
92025	WTEB	Bulgaria	Oscar Wilde
92026	WNTR	CE	Britten
92027	WTEB	Bulgaria	George Eliot
92028	GBET	CO	Saint Saëns
92029	WNWX	CE	Dante
92030	WTAE	CE	Ashford
92031	WNTR	CE	IMechE Railway Division
92032	GBET	CO	
92033	PTXX	CO	Berlioz
92034	WTEB	Bulgaria	Kipling
92035	WNWX	CE	Mendelssohn
92036	WTAE	CE	Bertolt Brecht
92037	WTAE	CE	Sullivan
92038	GBET	CO	Voltaire
92039	WTAE	CE	Johann Strauss
92040	PTXX	CO	Goethe
92041	WTAE	CE	Vaughan Williams
92042	WTHE	CE	
92043	GBET	CO	Debussy
92044	GBET	CO	Couperin
92045	PTXX	LB	Chaucer
92046	PTXX	LB	Sweelinck

CLASS 21 VOSSLOH G1206 TYPE 3 B-B

Built: 2004-2006
Weight: 87.3 tonnes
Maximum Tractive Effort: 57,000 lbf
Transmission: Voith L5r4zU2

Maximum Speed: 62 mph
Engine: Caterpillar 2000 hp
Wheel Diameter: 1000 mm
Route Availability:

FB1544(21544)		DL	FB1547(21547)	WLAN	DL
FB1545(21545)		DL	FB1610(21610)	WLAN	DL
FB1546(21546)	WLAN	DL	FB1611(21611)	WLAN	DL

Note: The above locos are normally only seen in Mainland Europe.

EUROTUNNEL LOCOMOTIVES

CLASS 21 MaK Bo - Bo

Built: 1992/93
Weight: 84 tonnes
Maximum Tractive Effort: 74,000 lbf

Maximum Speed: 47 mph
Transmission: Four ABB Traction Motors
Wheel Diameter: 1000 mm

Registered as 21901-21907

0001	CO	0003	CO	0005	CO	0007	CO
0002	CO	0004	CO	0006	CO		

CLASS 0 B

Built: 1989/90 rebuilt 1993/94
Engine: Deutz 200 hp
Maximum Tractive Effort:

Maximum Speed: 30 mph
Transmission: Mechanical
Wheel Diameter:

0031	CO	FRANCES	0035	CO	MARY	0039	CO	PACITA
0032	CO	ELISABETH	0036	CO	LAWRENCE	0040	CO	JILL
0033	CO	SILKE	0037	CO	LYDIE	0041	CO	KIM
0034	CO	AMANDA	0038	CO	JENNY	0042	CO	NICOLE

CLASS 9/0 BRUSH EUROSHUTTLE Bo - Bo - Bo

Built: 1992-2002 **Maximum Speed:** 100 mph
Weight: 132 tonnes **Route Availability:** Channel Tunnel Only
Maximum Tractive Effort: 90000 lbf **Wheel Diameter:** 1090 mm
Transmission: 6 ABB Traction Motors **Voltage:** 25 kV AC Overhead

9005	CO	JESSYE NORMAN	9024	CO	GOTTHARD 1882
9007	CO	DAME JOAN SUTHERLAND	9026	CO	FURKATUNNEL 1982
9011	CO	JOSÉ VAN DAM	9029	CO	THOMAS ALLEN
9013	CO	MARIA CALLAS	9033	CO	MONTSERRAT CABALLÉ
9015	CO	LÖTSCHBERG 1913	9036	CO	ALAIN FONDARY
9018	CO	WILHELMENA FERNANDEZ	9037	CO	GABRIEL BACQUIER
9022	CO	DAME JANET BAKER			

9/7 Freight Shuttle Locos 9701-9707 Built 2001/02

9701 CO	9705 CO	9712(9102)CO	9716(9106)CO	9720(9110)CO
9702 CO	9706 CO	9713(9103)CO	9717(9107)CO	9721(9111)CO
9703 CO	9707 CO	9714(9104)CO	9718(9108)CO	9722(9112)CO
9704 CO	9711(9101)CO	9715(9105)CO	9719(9109)CO	9723(9113)CO

9/8 (upgraded to 9387hp from 2004 onwards and renumbered from Class 9/0)

9801	CO	LESLEY GARRETT	9820	CO	NICOLAÏ GHIAUROV
9802	CO	STUART BURROWS	9821	CO	TERESA BERGANZA
9803	CO	BENJAMIN LUXON	9823	CO	DAME ELISABETH LEGGE-SCHWARZKOPF
9804	CO	VICTORIA DE LOS ANGELES			
9806	CO	REGINE CRESPIN	9825	CO	
9808	CO	ELISABETH SODERSTROM	9827	CO	BARBARA HENDRICKS
9809	CO	FRANCOISE POLLET	9828	CO	DAME KIRI TE KANAWA
9810	CO	JEAN - PHILIPPE COURTIS	9831	CO	
9812	CO	LUCIANO PAVAROTTI	9832	CO	RENATA TEBALDI
9814	CO	LUCIA POPP	9834	CO	MIRELLA FRENI
9816	CO	WILLARD WHITE	9835	CO	NICOLAÏ GEDDA
9817	CO	JOSÉ CARRERAS	9838	CO	HILDEGARD BEHRENS
9819	CO	MARIA EWING	9840	CO	

London Underground Battery/Electric Locos

97715	L15	MBEL	WR	97725	L25	MBEL	WR	97746	L46	MBEL	WR
97716	L16	MBEL	WR	97726	L26	MBEL	WR	97747	L47	MBEL	WR
97717	L17	MBEL	WR	97727	L27	MBEL	WR	97748	L48	MBEL	WR
97718	L18	MBEL	WR	97728	L28	MBEL	WR	97749	L49	MBEL	WR
97719	L19	MBEL	WR	97729	L29	MBEL	WR	97750	L50	MBEL	WR
97720	L20	MBEL	WR	97730	L30	MBEL	WR	97751	L51	MBEL	WR
97721	L21	MBEL	WR	97731	L31	MBEL	WR	97752	L52	MBEL	WR
97722	L22	MBEL	WR	97732	L32	MBEL	WR	97753	L53	MBEL	WR
97723	L23	MBEL	WR	97744	L44	MBEL	WR	97754	L54	MBEL	WR
97724	L24	MBEL	WR	97745	L45	MBEL	WR				

MANCHESTER METROLINK (operated by RATP Dev UK)

Operates on a 750v D.C. overhead system in and around Manchester with lines from Bury to Altrincham. Piccadilly to Altrincham. Bury to Droylsden extended to Ashton-under-Lyne by early 2014. Eccles to Piccadilly. MediaCityUK to Cornbrook. Chorlton St Werburgh's road to Shaw and Crompton extended to Oldham & Rochdale town centres by 2014 and from Chorlton St Werburgh's road to East Didsbury by summer 2013 and Manchester Airport by the summer of 2016. Depots at Queens Road and Trafford Bar.

1001s	(runs with 1025 when required)	1017	
1002		1018s	
1003		1019s	
1004s	VANS. The Original since 1966.	1020s	
1005s		1021	
1006s	VANS. The Original since 1966.	1022	POPPY APPEAL
1007	EAST LANCASHIRE RAILWAY	1023	
1008s		1024	
1009		1025s	(converted into ice breaker)
1010s		1026	
1011s	VANS. The Original since 1966.	2001	
1012		2002	
1013		2003	
1014		2004	
1015s		2005	
1016		2006	

Note: 1001/02/04-26 and 2001/03/04 all have aquamarine doors and roofline stripe. 1003 is now painted in Silver and Yellow livery with black doors. 1001-17/21-26 modified for use on Phase 2 (Eccles Line). All fitted with the new style destination boxes.

M5000 trams in a Silver and Yellow livery. Up to 3063 had been delivered by the end of January 2013 and 3001 to 3049 and 3060 were in service by early February 2013.

3001	3010	3021	3032
3002	3011	3022	3033
3003	3012	3023	3034
3004	3013	3024	3035
3005	3014	3025	3036
3006	3015	3026	3037
3007	3016	3027	3038
3008	3017	3028	3039
3009 Coronation Street	3018	3029	3040
50th Anniversary	3019	3030	3041
1960-2010	3020	3031	3042

3043	3056	3069	3082
3044	3057	3070	3083
3045	3058	3071	3084
3046	3059	3072	3085
3047	3060	3073	3086
3048	3061	3074	3087
3049	3062	3075	3088
3050	3063	3076	3089
3051	3064	3077	3090
3052	3065	3078	3091
3053	3066	3079	3092
3054	3067	3080	3093
3055	3068	3081	3094

MIDLAND METRO (operated by Travel West Midlands Limited)

Operates between Birmingham Snow Hill and Wolverhampton St Georges using a 750V D.C. overhead system. An extension under construction from Snow Hill to Stephenson Street by New Street Station is due to be completed in 2015. 20 new CAF trams due in service from 2014 will replace the present 16. Depot at Wednesbury will be extended.

01s		09	JEFF ASTLE
02		10	JOHN STANLEY WEBB
03	RAY LEWIS	11	THERESA STEWART
04	SIR FRANK WHITTLE	12	
05	SISTER DORA	13	ANTHONY NOLAN
06	ALAN GARNER	14	JIM EAMES
07	BILLY WRIGHT	15	AGENORIA
08	JOSEPH CHAMBERLAIN	16	GERWYN JOHN

NOTTINGHAM EXPRESS TRANSIT (operated by Tramlink Nottingham)

Operates on a 750v D.C. overhead system from Nottingham Station Street to Hucknall & Phoenix park & ride near to the M1. Work on extensions to Chilwell via Beeston approximately 6.2 miles and Clifton via Wilford approx.4.6 miles is now underway for completion by late 2014. 22 additional Citadis trams on order from Alstom.
Depot at Wilkinson Street, Basford.

201	Torvill and Dean	209	Sid Standard
202	D H Lawrence	210	Sir Jesse Boot
203	William "Bengigo" Thompson	211	Robin Hood
204	Erica Beardsmore	212	William Booth
205	Lord Byron	213	Mary Potter
206	Angela Alcock	214	Dennis McCarthy, MBE
207	Mavis Worthington	215	Brian Clough
208	Dinah Minton		

TYNE & WEAR METRO (operated by DB Regio for Nexus (Tyne & Wear Passenger Transport Executive) Operates on a 1500V D.C. overhead system over 48 miles.
Depot at South Gosforth. (Allocated TOP's numbers 994001-994090)

4001	4024	4047	4069
4002	4025	4048	4070
4003	4026 George Stephenson	4049	4071
4004	4027	4050	4072
4005	4028	4051	4073 Danny Marshall
4006	4029	4052	4074
4007	4030	4053	4075
4008	4031	4054	4076
4009	4032	4055	4077 Robert Stephenson
4010	4033	4056	4078 Ellen Wilkinson
4011	4034	4057	4079
4012	4035	4058	4080
4013	4036	4059	4081
4014	4037	4060 Thomas Bewick	4082
4015	4038	4061	4083
4016	4039	4062	4084
4017	4040	4063	4085
4018	4041	4064 Michael Campbell	4086
4019	4042	4065 DAME Catherine Cookson	4087
4020	4043		4088
4021	4044	4066	4089
4022	4045	4067	4090
4023	4046	4068	

Hunslet Battery Electric Locos

BL1	BL2	BL3

LONDON TRAMLINK (operated by Transport for London)

Operates over 18½ miles through Croydon to Wimbledon, New Addington and Beckenham Jct/Elmers End on a 750V D.C. overhead system. Depot at Therapia Lane in Croydon.

2530	2538	2546	2553
2531	2539	2547	2554
2532	2540	2548	2555
2533	2541	2549	2556
2534	2542	2550	2557
2535	2543	2551	2558
2536	2544	2552	2559
2537	2545		

2535 STEPHEN PARASCANDOLO 1980-2007

DOCKLANDS LIGHT RAILWAY (owned by DLR, operated by Serco Docklands)

Operates in parts of London's East End between Bank, Tower Gateway to Stratford, Beckton, Lewisham and King George V and Woolwich Arsenal and from Stratford International to Canning Town on a 750V D.C third rail system over a total of approximately 23 miles
Depots at Beckton and Poplar

01	36	66	96	127
02	37	67	97	128
03	38	68	98	129
04	39	69	99	130
05	40	70	101	131
06	41	71	102	132
07	42	72	103	133
08	43	73	104	134
09	44	74	105	135
10	45	75	106	136
11	46	76	107	137
12	47	77	108	138
13	48	78	109	139
14	49	79	110	140
15	50*	80	111	141
16	51	81	112	142
22	52	82	113	143
23	53	83	114	144
24	54	84	115	145
25	55	85	116	146
26	56	86	117	147
27	57	87	118	148
28	58	88	119	149
29	59	89	120	150
30	60	90	121	151
31	61	91	122	152
32	62	92	123	153
33	63	93	124	154
34	64	94	125	155
35	65	95	126	

*The Countess of Wessex.

STAGECOACH SUPERTRAM SHEFFIELD (7 tram/trains ordered for Rotherham extension)

Operates on a 750V D.C. overhead system over 18 miles using three routes in and around Sheffield. Extensions are planned to Rotherham, Dore and Ranmoor. Depot at Nunnery.

101	106	111	116	121
102	107	112	117	122
103	108	113	118	123
104	109	114	119	124
105	110	115	120	125

BLACKPOOL & FLEETWOOD TRAMWAY

Operates over 11½ miles between Starr Gate and Fleetwood on a 660V D.C overhead system. Depots at Rigby Road and Starr Gate.

Flexity Swift 2 trams

001	005	008	011	014
002	006	009	012	015
003	007	010	013	016
004				

002 Alderman E.E. Wynne.

T2	(682)	642s		685s	(T5)	707	(244)	718	(255)
230	(604)	648	(651)	686s	(T6)	709	(246)	719	(256)
272	(672)	675s	(275)	700	(237)	711	(248)	720s	(257)
600	(225)	676s	(276)	701	(238)	713	(250)	723	(260)
602s	(227)	680*	(280)	706	(243)	717	(254)	724	(261)
631	(294)								

*sold.

230 GEORGE FORMBY OBE. 600 THE DUCHESS OF CORNWALL. 706 PRINCESS ALICE.
717 PHILLIP R THORPE. 719 DONNA'S DREAM HOUSE.

ILLUMINATED CARS

733(209)	Western Train Loco and Tender	736(170)	HMS Blackpool
734(174)	Western Train coach	737(633)	Trawler

WORKS CARS

260(291)	Crane car & rail carrier (oou)
750	Reel Wagon
754	Overhead Line Car
938	Overhead Inspection Car (out of use)
939	Road/Rail vehicle
Crab	Starr Gate Shunter

VINTAGE CARS

Blackpool & Fleetwood 40
Blackpool 147 Michael Airey
Blackpool 660, Coronation Class
Bolton 66

STRATHCLYDE PTE UNDERGROUND

Operates on a circular underground line over approx 6.2 miles in Glasgow on a 600V D.C. third rail system. Depot at Broomloan.

101	110	118	126	201
102	111	119	127	202
103	112	120	128	203
104	113	121	129	204
105	114	122	130	205
106	115	123	131	206
107	116	124	132	207
108	117	125	133	208
109				

BATTERY ELECTRIC LOCOS

L2	LOBEY DOSSER	L4	EL FIDELDO	L7
L3	RANK BAJIN	L6		

EDINBURGH TRAMS

Construction underway on the streets of Edinburgh and a full revenue service is expected to be operational by the summer of 2014. Planned operation was to be over 11½ miles from Edinburgh Airport to Newhaven but has now been shortened to approximately 8¾ miles to terminate at York Place close to St Marys Cathedral. Depot at Gogar.
All 27 trams ordered had been delivered by the end of 2012

251	257	263	268	273
252	258	264	269	274
253	259	265	270	275
254	260	266	271	276
255	261	267	272	277
256	262			

DIESEL MULTIPLE UNITS

Operating Codes used in the Multiple Unit Headings

B	Brake	M	Motor
C	Composite	O	Open
DM	Driving Motor	P	Pantograph(when fitted to trailer vehicle)
DT	Driving Trailer	RB/RMB	Fitted with Buffet/Minature Buffet
D at end	Disabled facilities	S	Standard
F	First	T	Trailer
H	Handbrake	V	Van
L	fitted with Lavatory	W	Wheelchair facilities

Example:- DMCD = Driving Motor Composite with Disabled facilities

Heritage Diesel Multiple Units

Class 121 Pressed Steel "Suburban"

	DMBS			DMBS	
121020	55020	AL	121034	55034	AL
121032	55032	CF			

note: allocated set numbers are not always carried in full

Parry People Mover

Class 139 PPM60

139001	39001	SJ	139002	39002	SJ

Class 142 Leyland/BREL Railbus

		DMS	DMSL
142001	NH	55542	55592
142002	CF	55543	55593
142003	NH	55544	55594
142004	NH	55545	55595
142005	NH	55546	55596
142006	CF	55547	55597
142007	NH	55548	55598
142009	NH	55550	55600
142010	CF	55551	55601
142011	NH	55552	55602
142012	NH	55553	55603
142013	NH	55554	55604
142014	NH	55555	55605
142015	HT	55556	55606
142016	HT	55557	55607
142017	HT	55558	55608
142018	HT	55559	55609
142019	HT	55560	55610
142020	HT	55561	55611
142021	HT	55562	55612
142022	HT	55563	55613
142023	HT	55564	55614
142024	HT	55565	55615
142025	HT	55566	55616
142026	HT	55567	55617
142027	HT	55568	55618
142028	NH	55569	55619
142029	HT	55570	55620
142030	NH	55571	55621
142031	NH	55572	55622
142032	NH	55573	55623
142033	NH	55574	55624
142034	NH	55575	55625
142035	NH	55576	55626
142036	NH	55577	55627
142037	NH	55578	55628
142038	NH	55579	55629
142039	NH	55580	55630
142040	NH	55581	55631
142041	NH	55582	55632
142042	NH	55583	55633
142043	NH	55584	55634

		DMS	DMSL
142044	NH	55585	55635
142045	NH	55586	55636
142046	NH	55587	55637
142047	NH	55588	55638
142048	NH	55589	55639
142049	NH	55590	55640
142050	HT	55591	55641
142051	NH	55701	55747
142052	NH	55702	55748
142053	NH	55703	55749
142054	NH	55704	55750
142055	NH	55705	55751
142056	NH	55706	55752
142057	NH	55707	55753
142058	NH	55708	55754
142060	NH	55710	55756
142061	NH	55711	55757
142062	NH	55712	55758
142063	NH	55713	55759
142064	HT	55714	55760
142065	HT	55715	55761
142066	HT	55716	55762
142067	HT	55717	55763
142068	HT	55718	55764
142069	CF	55719	55765
142070	HT	55720	55766
142071	HT	55721	55767
142072	CF	55722	55768
142073*	CF	55723	55769
142074	CF	55724	55770
142075	CF	55725	55771
142076	CF	55726	55772
142077	CF	55727	55773
142078	HT	55728	55774
142079	HT	55729	55775
142080	CF	55730	55776
142081	CF	55731	55777
142082	CF	55732	55778
142083	CF	55733	55779
142084	HT	55734	55780
142085	CF	55735	55781
142086	HT	55736	55782

142087	HT	55737	55783
142088	HT	55738	55784
142089	HT	55739	55785
142090	HT	55740	55786
142091	HT	55741	55787
142092	HT	55742	55788
142093	HT	55743	55789
142094	HT	55744	55790
142095	HT	55745	55791
142096	HT	55746	55792

*142073 Myfanwy.

Class 143/6 Alexander/Barclay Railbus

		DMS	DMSL
143601	CF	55642	55667
143602	CF	55651	55668
143603	EX	55658	55669
143604	CF	55645	55670
143605	CF	55646	55671
143606	CF	55647	55672
143607	CF	55648	55673
143608	CF	55649	55674
143609*	CF	55650	55675
143610	CF	55643	55676
143611	EX	55652	55677
143612	EX	55653	55678
143614	CF	55655	55680
143616	CF	55657	55682
143617	EX	55644	55683
143618	EX	55659	55684
143619	EX	55660	55685
143620	EX	55661	55686
143621	EX	55662	55687
143622	CF	55663	55688
143623	CF	55664	55689
143624	CF	55665	55690
143625	CF	55666	55691

*143609 Sir Tom Jones

Class 144 Alexander/BREL Railbus

		DMS	MS	DMSL
144001*	NL	55801		55824
144002	NL	55802		55825
144003	NL	55803		55826
144004	NL	55804		55827
144005	NL	55805		55828
144006	NL	55806		55829
144007	NL	55807		55830
144008	NL	55808		55831
144009	NL	55809		55832
144010	NL	55810		55833
144011	NL	55811		55834
144012	NL	55812		55835
144013	NL	55813		55836
144014	NL	55814	55850	55837
144015	NL	55815	55851	55838
144016	NL	55816	55852	55839
144017	NL	55817	55853	55840
144018	NL	55818	55854	55841
144019	NL	55819	55855	55842
144020	NL	55820	55856	55843
144021	NL	55821	55857	55844
144022	NL	55822	55858	55845
144023	NL	55823	55859	55846

*144001 THE PENISTONE LINE PARTNERSHIP

Class 150/0 BREL York Prototype Sprinter

		DMSL	MS	DMS
150001	RG	55200	55400	55300
150002	RG	55201	55401	55301

Class 150/1 BREL Derby Sprinter

		DMSL	DMS
150101	PM	52101	57101
150102	PM	52102	57102
150103	NH	52103	57103
150104	PM	52104	57104
150105	TS	52105	57105
150106	PM	52106	57106
150107	TS	52107	57107
150108	PM	52108	57108
150109	TS	52109	57109
150110	NH	52110	57110
150111	NH	52111	57111
150112	NH	52112	57112
150113	NH	52113	57113
150114	NH	52114	57114
150115	NH	52115	57115
150116	NH	52116	57116
150117	NH	52117	57117
150118	NH	52118	57118
150119	NH	52119	57119
150120	EX	52120	57120
150122	EX	52122	57122
150123	EX	52123	57123
150124	EX	52124	57124
150125	EX	52125	57125
150126	EX	52126	57126

		DMSL	DMS	DMS
150128	EX	52128	57128	
150129	EX	52129	57129	
150130	EX	52130	57130	
150131	EX	52131	57131	
150132	NH	52132	57132	
150133	NH	52133	57133	
150134	NH	52134	57134	
150135	NH	52135	57135	
150136	NH	52136	57136	
150137	NH	52137	57137	
150138	NH	52138	57138	
150139	NH	52139	57139	
150140	NH	52140	57140	
150141	NH	52141	57141	
150142	NH	52142	57142	
150143	NH	52143	57143	
150144	NH	52144	57144	
150145	NH	52145	57145	
150146	NH	52146	57146	
150147	NH	52147	57147	
150148	NH	52148	57148	
150149	NH	52149	57149	
150150	NH	52150	57150	
150921	PM	52121	57212	57121
150927	PM	52127	57209	57127

150125 Heart of Wessex CRP. 150129 Devon and Cornwall Rail Partnership.
150130 Severnside Community Rail Partnership.

Class 150/2 BREL Derby Sprinter

		DMSL	DMS
150201	NH	52201	57201
150202	PM	52202	57202
150203	NH	52203	57203
150204	NH	52204	57204
150205	NH	52205	57205
150206	NH	52206	57206
150207	NH	52207	57207
150208	CF	52208	57208
150210	NH	52210	57210
150211	NH	52211	57211
150213	CF	52213	57213
150214	NH	52214	57214
150215	NH	52215	57215
150216	PM	52216	57216
150217	CF	52217	57217
150218	NH	52218	57218
150219	PM	52219	57219
150220	NH	52220	57220
150221	PM	52221	57221
150222	NH	52222	57222
150223	NH	52223	57223
150224	NH	52224	57224
150225	NH	52225	57225
150226	NH	52226	57226
150227	CF	52227	57227
150228	NH	52228	57228
150229	CF	52229	57229
150230	CF	52230	57230
150231	CF	52231	57231
150232	PM	52232	57232
150233	PM	52233	57233
150234	PM	52234	57234
150235	CF	52235	57235
150236	CF	52236	57236
150237	CF	52237	57237
150238	PM	52238	57238
150239	PM	52239	57239
150240	CF	52240	57240
150241	CF	52241	57241
150242	CF	52242	57242
150243	PM	52243	57243
150244	PM	52244	57244

		DMSL	DMS
150245	CF	52245	57245
150246	PM	52246	57246
150247	PM	52247	57247
150248	PM	52248	57248
150249	PM	52249	57249
150250	CF	52250	57250
150251	CF	52251	57251
150252	CF	52252	57252
150253	CF	52253	57253
150254	CF	52254	57254
150255	CF	52255	57255
150256	CF	52256	57256
150257	CF	52257	57257
150258	CF	52258	57258
150259	CF	52259	57259
150260	CF	52260	57260
150261	PM	52261	57261
150262	CF	52262	57262
150263	PM	52263	57263
150264	CF	52264	57264
150265	PM	52265	57265
150266	PM	52266	57266
150267	CF	52267	57267
150268	NH	52268	57268
150269	NH	52269	57269
150270	NH	52270	57270
150271	NH	52271	57271
150272	NH	52272	57272
150273	NH	52273	57273
150274	NH	52274	57274
150275	NH	52275	57275
150276	NH	52276	57276
150277	NH	52277	57277
150278	CF	52278	57278
150279	CF	52279	57279
150280	CF	52280	57280
150281	CF	52281	57281
150282	CF	52282	57282
150283	CF	52283	57283
150284	CF	52284	57284
150285	CF	52285	57285

Class 153/0 Leyland Super Sprinter single car converted from class 155

		DMSL
153301	NL	52301
153302	NM	52302
153303	CF	52303
153304	NL	52304
153305	PM	52305
153306	NC	52306
153307	NL	52307
153308	NM	52308
153309*	NC	52309
153310	NM	52310
153311	NM	52311
153312	CF	52312
153313	NM	52313
153314	NC	52314
153315	NL	52315
153316	NH	52316
153317	NL	52317
153318	PM	52318
153319	NM	52319
153320	CF	52320
153321	NM	52321
153322*	NC	52322
153323	CF	52323
153324	NH	52324
153325	EX	52325
153326	NM	52326
153327	CF	52327
153328	NL	52328
153329	EX	52329
153330	NH	52330
153331	NL	52331
153332	NH	52332
153333	EX	52333
153334	TS	52334
153335*	NC	52335

		DMSL
153351	NL	57351
153352	NL	57352
153353	CF	57353
153354	TS	57354
153355	NM	57355
153356	TS	57356
153357	NM	57357
153358	NH	57358
153359	NH	57359
153360	NH	57360
153361	PM	57361
153362*	CF	57362
153363	NH	57363
153364	TS	57364
153365	TS	57365
153366	TS	57366
153367	CF	57367
153368	PM	57368
153369	PM	57369
153370	PM	57370
153371	TS	57371
153372	PM	57372
153373	PM	57373
153374	NM	57374
153375	TS	57375
153376	NM	57376
153377	PM	57377
153378	NL	57378
153379	NM	57379
153380	PM	57380
153381	NM	57381
153382	PM	57382
153383	NM	57383
153384	NM	57334
153385	NM	57385

*153309 GERARD FIENNES´. *153322 BENJAMIN BRITTEN. *153335 MICHAEL PALIN.
*153362 Dylan Thomas 1914-1953.

Class 155 Leyland Super Sprinter

		DMSL	DMS
155341	NL	52341	57341
155342	NL	52342	57342
155343	NL	52343	57343
155344	NL	52344	57344
155345	NL	52345	57345
155346	NL	52346	57346
155347	NL	52347	57347

Class 156 Metro-Cammell Super Sprinter

		DMSL	DMS
156401	DY	52401	57401
156402	NC	52402	57402
156403	DY	52403	57403
156404	DY	52404	57404
156405	DY	52405	57405
156406	DY	52406	57406
156407	NC	52407	57407
156408	DY	52408	57408
156409*	NC	52409	57409
156410	DY	52410	57410
156411	DY	52411	57411
156412	NC	52412	57412
156413	DY	52413	57413
156414	DY	52414	57414
156415	DY	52415	57415
156416*	NC	52416	57416
156417	NC	52417	57417
156418	NC	52418	57418
156419	NC	52419	57419
156420*	AN	52420	57420
156421	AN	52421	57421
156422	NC	52422	57422
156423	AN	52423	57423
156424	AN	52424	57424
156425	AN	52425	57425
156426	AN	52426	57426
156427	AN	52427	57427
156428	AN	52428	57428
156429	AN	52429	57429
156430	CK	52430	57430
156431	CK	52431	57431
156432	CK	52432	57432
156433	CK	52433	57433
156434	CK	52434	57434
156435	CK	52435	57435
156436	CK	52436	57436
156437	CK	52437	57437
156438*	HT	52438	57438
156439	CK	52439	57439
156440*	AN	52440	57440
156441*	AN	52441	57441
156442	CK	52442	57442
156443	HT	52443	57443
156444*	HT	52444	57444
156445	CK	52445	57445
156446	CK	52446	57446
156447	CK	52447	57447

		DMSL	DMS
156448	HT	52448	57448
156449	CK	52449	57449
156450	CK	52450	57450
156451	HT	52451	57451
156452	AN	52452	57452
156453	CK	52453	57453
156454	HT	52454	57454
156455	AN	52455	57455
156456	CK	52456	57456
156457	CK	52457	57457
156458	CK	52458	57458
156459*	AN	52459	57459
156460*	AN	52460	57460
156461	AN	52461	57461
156462	CK	52462	57462
156463	HT	52463	57463
156464	AN	52464	57464
156465	CK	52465	57465
156466*	AN	52466	57466
156467	CK	52467	57467
156468	AN	52468	57468
156469	HT	52469	57469
156470	DY	52470	57470
156471	AN	52471	57471
156472	AN	52472	57472
156473	DY	52473	57473
156474	CK	52474	57474
156475	HT	52475	57475
156476	CK	52476	57476
156477	CK	52477	57477
156478	CK	52478	57478
156479	HT	52479	57479
156480	HT	52480	57480
156481	HT	52481	57481
156482	AN	52482	57482
156483	AN	52483	57483
156484	HT	52484	57484
156485	CK	52485	57485
156486	AN	52486	57486
156487	AN	52487	57487
156488	AN	52488	57488
156489	AN	52489	57489
156490	HT	52490	57490
156491	AN	52491	57491
156492	CK	52492	57492
156493	CK	52493	57493
156494	CK	52494	57494

156495	CK	52495	57495
156496	CK	52496	57496
156497	DY	52497	57497
156498	DY	52498	57498
156499	CK	52499	57499
156500	CK	52500	57500
156501	CK	52501	57501
156502	CK	52502	57502
156503	CK	52503	57503
156504	CK	52504	57504
156505	CK	52505	57505
156506	CK	52506	57506
156507	CK	52507	57507
156508	CK	52508	57508
156509	CK	52509	57509
156510	CK	52510	57510
156511	CK	52511	57511
156512	CK	52512	57512
156513	CK	52513	57513
156514	CK	52514	57514

*156409 Cromer Pier Seaside Special. *156416 Saint Edmund. *156420 LA'AL RATTY Ravenglass & Eskdale Railway. *156438 Timothy Hackworth. *156440 George Bradshaw. *156441 William Huskisson MP. *156444 Councillor Bill Cameron. *156459 Benny Rothman-The Manchester Rambler. *156460 Driver John Axon G.C. *156466 Gracie Fields.

Class 158 BREL Derby Express

		DMSL/ •DMCL	MSL	DMSL
158701	IS	52701•		57701
158702	IS	52702•		57702
158703	IS	52703•		57703
158704	IS	52704•		57704
158705	IS	52705•		57705
158706	IS	52706•		57706
158707*	IS	52707•		57707
158708	IS	52708•		57708
158709	IS	52709•		57709
158710	IS	52710•		57710
158711	IS	52711•		57711
158712	IS	52712•		57712
158713	IS	52713•		57713
158714	IS	52714•		57714
158715*	IS	52715•		57715
158716	IS	52716•		57716
158717	IS	52717•		57717
158718	IS	52718•		57718
158719	IS	52719•		57719
158720*	IS	52720•		57720
158721	IS	52721•		57721
158722	IS	52722•		57722
158723	IS	52723•		57723
158724	IS	52724•		57724
158725	IS	52725•		57725
158726	HA	52726•		57726
158727	HA	52727•		57727
158728	HA	52728•		57728
158729	HA	52729•		57729
158730	HA	52730•		57730
158731	HA	52731•		57731
158732	HA	52732•		57732
158733	HA	52733•		57733
158734	HA	52734•		57734
158735	HA	52735•		57735
158736	HA	52736•		57736
158738	HA	52738•		57738
158739	HA	52739•		57739
158740	HA	52740•		57740
158741	HA	52741•		57741
158752	NL	52752	58716	57752
158753	NL	52753	58710	57753
158754	NL	52754	58708	57754
158755	NL	52755	58702	57755
158756	NL	52756	58712	57756
158757	NL	52757	58706	57757
158758	NL	52758	58714	57758
158759	NL	52759	58713	57759
158763	PM	52763•		57763
158766	PM	52766•		57766
158770	NM	52770•		57770
158773	NM	52773•		57773
158774	NM	52774•		57774
158777	NM	52777•		57777
158780	NM	52780		57780
158782	HA	52782		57782
158783	NM	52783		57783
158784*	NL	52784		57784

158785	NM	52785		57785
158786	HA	52786•		57786
158787	NL	52787		57787
158788	NM	52788		57788
158789	HA	52789•		57789
158790	NL	52790		57790
158791*	NL	52791		57791
158792	NL	52792		57792
158793	NL	52793		57793
158794	NL	52794		57794
158795	NL	52795		57795
158796*	NL	52796		57796
158797*	NL	52797		57797
158798	PM	52798•	58715	57798
158799	NM	52799•		57799
158806	NM	52806•		57806
158810	NM	52810•		57810
158812	NM	52812•		57812
158813	NM	52813•		57813
158815	NL	52815		57815
158816	NL	52816		57816
158817	NL	52817		57817
158818	MN	52818		57818
158819	MN	52819		57819
158820	MN	52820		57820
158821	MN	52821		57821
158822	MN	52822		57822
158823	MN	52823		57823
158824	MN	52824		57824
158825	MN	52825		57825
158826	MN	52826		57826
158827	MN	52827		57827
158828	MN	52828		57828
158829	MN	52829		57829
158830	MN	52830		57830
158831	MN	52831		57831
158832	MN	52832		57832
158833	MN	52833		57833
158834	MN	52834		57834
158835	MN	52835		57835
158836	MN	52836		57836
158837	MN	52837		57837
158838	MN	52838		57838
158839	MN	52839		57839

158840	MN	52840	57840
158841	MN	52841	57841
158842	NL	52842	57842
158843	NL	52843	57843
158844	NL	52844	57844
158845	NL	52845	57845
158846	NM	52846	57846
158847	NM	52847	57847
158848	NL	52848	57848
158849	NL	52849	57849
158850	NL	52850	57850
158851	NL	52851	57851
158852	NM	52852	57852
158853	NL	52853	57853
158854	NM	52854	57854
158855	NL	52855	57855
158856	NM	52856	57856
158857	NM	52857	57857
158858	NM	52858	57858
158859	NL	52859	57859
158860*	NL	52860	57860
158861	NL	52861	57861
158862	NM	52862	57862
158863	NM	52863	57863
158864	NM	52864	57864
158865	NM	52865	57865
158866	NM	52866	57866
158867	HA	52867	57867
158868	HA	52868	57868
158869	HA	52869	57869
158870	HA	52870	57870
158871	HA	52871	57871
158872	NL	52872	57872
158880	SA	52737•	57737
158881	SA	52742•	57742
158882	SA	52743•	57743
158883	SA	52744•	57744
158884	SA	52772•	57772
158885	SA	52775•	57775
158886	SA	52779•	57779
158887	SA	52781•	57781
158888	SA	52802•	57802
158889	SA	52808•	57808
158890	SA	52814•	57814

*158707 FAR NORTH LINE 125th ANNIVERSARY. *158715 Haymarket.

*158720 Inverness & Nairn Railway-150 years. *158784 Barbara Castle. *158791 County of Nottinghamshire.

*158796 Fred Trueman Cricketing Legend. *158797 Jane Tomlinson. *158860 Ian Dewhirst.

Class 158/9 BREL Derby Express

		DMSL	DMS
158901	NL	52901	57901
158902	NL	52902	57902
158903	NL	52903	57903
158904	NL	52904	57904
158905	NL	52905	57905
158906	NL	52906	57906
158907	NL	52907	57907
158908	NL	52908	57908
158909	NL	52909	57909
158910*	NL	52910	57910

*William Wilberforce

Class 158/9 BREL Derby Express

		DMS	DMS	DMS
158950	PM	57751	52761	57761
158951	PM	52751	52764	57764
158952	PM	57745	52762	57762
158953	PM	52745	52750	57750
158954	PM	57747	52760	57760
158955	PM	52747	52765	57765
158956	PM	52748	52768	57768
158957	PM	57748	52771	57771
158958	PM	57746	52776	57776
158959	PM	52746	52778	57778
158960	PM	57749	52769	57769
158961	PM	52749	52767	57767
158962				

Class 159/0 BREL Derby Express

		DMCL	MSL	DMSL
159001	SA	52873	58718	57873
159002	SA	52874	58719	57874
159003	SA	52875	58720	57875
159004	SA	52876	58721	57876
159005	SA	52877	58722	57877
159006	SA	52878	58723	57878
159007	SA	52879	58724	57879
159008	SA	52880	58725	57880
159009	SA	52881	58726	57881
159010	SA	52882	58727	57882
159011	SA	52883	58728	57883
159012	SA	52884	58729	57884
159013	SA	52885	58730	57885
159014	SA	52886	58731	57886
159015	SA	52887	58732	57887
159016	SA	52888	58733	57888
159017	SA	52889	58734	57889
159018	SA	52890	58735	57890
159019	SA	52891	58736	57891
159020	SA	52892	58737	57892
159021	SA	52893	58738	57893
159022	SA	52894	58739	57894

*159002 CITY OF SALISBURY. *159003 TEMPLECOMBE. *159004 BASINGSTOKE AND DEANE. *159005 WEST OF ENGLAND LINE.

Class 159/1 BREL Derby Express

		DMCL	MSL	DMSL
159101	SA	52800	58717	57800
159102	SA	52803	58703	57803
159103	SA	52804	58704	57804
159104	SA	52805	58705	57805
159105	SA	52807	58707	57807
159106	SA	52809	58709	57809
159107	SA	52811	58711	57811
159108	SA	52801	58701	57801

159101 to 159108 renumbered from 158800/803/804/805/807/809/811 & 801

Class 165/0 BREL York Networker Turbo

		DMSL	DMS
165001	AL	58801	58834
165002	AL	58802	58835
165003	AL	58803	58836
165004	AL	58804	58837
165005	AL	58805	58838
165006	AL	58806	58839
165007	AL	58807	58840
165008	AL	58808	58841
165009	AL	58809	58842
165010	AL	58810	58843
165011	AL	58811	58844
165012	AL	58812	58845
165013	AL	58813	58846
165014	AL	58814	58847
165015	AL	58815	58848
165016	AL	58816	58849
165017	AL	58817	58850
165018	AL	58818	58851
165019	AL	58819	58852
165020	AL	58820	58853

		DMSL	MS	DMS
165021	AL	58821		58854
165022	AL	58822		58855
165023	AL	58867		58873
165024	AL	58868		58874
165025	AL	58869		58875
165026	AL	58870		58876
165027	AL	58871		58877
165028	AL	58872		58878
165029	AL	58823	55404	58856
165030	AL	58824	55405	58857
165031	AL	58825	55406	58858
165032	AL	58826	55407	58859
165033	AL	58827	55408	58860
165034	AL	58828	55409	58861
165035	AL	58829	55410	58862
165036	AL	58830	55411	58863
165037	AL	58831	55412	58864
165038	AL	58832	55413	58865
165039	AL	58833	55414	58866

Class 165/1 BREL York Network Turbo

		DMCL	MS	DMS
165101	RG	58916	55415	58953
165102	RG	58917	55416	58954
165103	RG	58918	55417	58955
165104	RG	58919	55418	58956
165105	RG	58920	55419	58957
165106	RG	58921	55420	58958
165107	RG	58922	55421	58959
165108	RG	58923	55422	58960
165109	RG	58924	55423	58961
165110	RG	58925	55424	58962
165111	RG	58926	55425	58963
165112	RG	58927	55426	58964
165113	RG	58928	55427	58965
165114	RG	58929	55428	58966
165116	RG	58931	55430	58968
165117	RG	58932	55431	58969
165118	RG	58879	58933	
165119	RG	58880	58934	

		DMCL	DMS
165120	RG	58881	58935
165121	RG	58882	58936
165122	RG	58883	58937
165123	RG	58884	58938
165124	RG	58885	58939
165125	RG	58886	58940
165126	RG	58887	58941
165127	RG	58888	58942
165128	RG	58889	58943
165129	RG	58890	58944
165130	RG	58891	58945
165131	RG	58892	58946
165132	RG	58893	58947
165133	RG	58894	58948
165134	RG	58895	58949
165135	RG	58896	58950
165136	RG	58897	58951
165137	RG	58898	58952

Odd vehicle 58930 ex 165115 at ZC.

Class 166 ABB Network Express Turbo

Unit	Depot	DMCL	MS	DMCL
166201	RG	58101	58601	58122
166202	RG	58102	58602	58123
166203	RG	58103	58603	58124
166204	RG	58104	58604	58125
166205	RG	58105	58605	58126
166206	RG	58106	58606	58127
166207	RG	58107	58607	58128
166208	RG	58108	58608	58129
166209	RG	58109	58609	58130
166210	RG	58110	58610	58131
166211	RG	58111	58611	58132
166212	RG	58112	58612	58133
166213	RG	58113	58613	58134
166214	RG	58114	58614	58135
166215	RG	58115	58615	58136
166216	RG	58116	58616	58137
166217	RG	58117	58617	58138
166218	RG	58118	58618	58139
166219	RG	58119	58619	58140
166220	RG	58120	58620	58141
166221	RG	58121	58621	58142

Class 168/0 Adtranz Clubman

Unit	Depot	DMSL	MSL	MS	DMSL
168001	AL	58151	58651	58451	58251
168002	AL	58152	58652	58452	58252
168003	AL	58153	58653	58453	58253
168004	AL	58154	58654	58454	58254
168005	AL	58155	58655	58455	58255

Class 168/1 Adtranz Clubman

Unit	Depot	DMSL	MS	MSL	DMSL
168106	AL	58156	58456	58756	58256
168107	AL	58157	58457	58757	58257
168108	AL	58158	58458		58258
168109	AL	58159	58459		58259
168110	AL	58160	58460		58260
168111	AL	58161	58461		58261
168112	AL	58162	58462		58262
168113	AL	58163	58463		58263

Class 168/2 Adtranz Clubman

Unit	Depot	DMSL	MS	MS	DMSL
168214	AL	58164	58464		58264
168215	AL	58165	58465	58365	58265
168216	AL	58166	58466	58366	58266
168217	AL	58167	58467	58367	58267
168218	AL	58168	58468		58268
168219	AL	58169	58469		58269

Class 170/1 Adtranz Turbostar

Unit	Depot	DMSL	MS	DMCL
170101	TS	50101	55101	79101
170102	TS	50102	55102	79102
170103	TS	50103	55103	79103
170104	TS	50104	55104	79104
170105	TS	50105	55105	79105
170106	TS	50106	55106	79106
170107	TS	50107	55107	79107
170108	TS	50108	55108	79108
170109	TS	50109	55109	79109
170110	TS	50110	55110	79110
170111	TS	50111		79111
170112	TS	50112		79112
170113	TS	50113		79113
170114	TS	50114		79114
170115	TS	50115		79115
170116	TS	50116		79116
170117	TS	50117		79117

Class 170/2 Adtranz Turbostar

		DMCL	MSL	DMSL
170201	NC	50201	56201	79201
170202	NC	50202	56202	79202
170203	NC	50203	56203	79203
170204	NC	50204	56204	79204
170205	NC	50205	56205	79205
170206	NC	50206	56206	79206
170207	NC	50207	56207	79207
170208	NC	50208	56208	79208

Class 170/2 Bombardier Turbostar

		DMSL	DMCL
170270	NC	50270	79270
170271	NC	50271	79271
170272	NC	50272	79272
170273	NC	50273	79273

Class 170/3 Adtranz/Bombardier Turbostar

		DMCL	DMCL
170301	XW	50301	79301
170302	XW	50302	79302
170303	XW	50303	79303
170304	XW	50304	79304
170305	XW	50305	79305
170306	XW	50306	79306
170307	XW	50307	79307
170308	XW	50308	79308

		DMCL	MSLRB •MC	DMCL •DMSL
170309	XW	50399		79399
170393	HA	50393	56393	79393•
170394	HA	50394	56394	79394•
170395	HA	50395	56395	79395•
170396	HA	50396	56396	79396•
170397	TS	50397	56397•	79397
170398	TS	50398	56398•	79398

Class 170/4 Adtranz/Bombardier Turbostar

		DMCL	MS	DMCL
170401*	HA	50401	56401	79401
170402	HA	50402	56402	79402
170403	HA	50403	56403	79403
170404	HA	50404	56404	79404
170405*	HA	50405	56405	79405
170406	HA	50406	56406	79406
170407*	HA	50407	56407	79407
170408	HA	50408	56408	79408
170409	HA	50409	56409	79409
170410	HA	50410	56410	79410
170411	HA	50411	56411	79411
170412	HA	50412	56412	79412
170413	HA	50413	56413	79413
170414	HA	50414	56414	79414
170415	HA	50415	56415	79415
170416	HA	50416	56416	79416
170417	HA	50417	56417	79417
170418	HA	50418	56418	79418
170419	HA	50419	56419	79419
170420	HA	50420	56420	79420
170421	HA	50421	56421	79421
170422	HA	50422	56422	79422
170423	HA	50423	56423	79423
170424	HA	50424	56424	79424
170425	HA	50425	56425	79425
170426	HA	50426	56426	79426
170427	HA	50427	56427	79427
170428	HA	50428	56428	79428
170429	HA	50429	56429	79429
170430	HA	50430	56430	79430
170431	HA	50431	56431	79431
170432	HA	50432	56432	79432
170433*	HA	50433	56433	79433
170434	HA	50434	56434	79434

		DMSL	MS	DMSL
170450	HA	50450	56450	79450
170451	HA	50451	56451	79451
170452	HA	50452	56452	79452
170453	HA	50453	56453	79453
170454	HA	50454	56454	79454
170455	HA	50455	56455	79455
170456	HA	50456	56456	79456
170457	HA	50457	56457	79457
170458	HA	50458	56458	79458
170459	HA	50459	56459	79459
170460	HA	50460	56460	79460
170461	HA	50461	56461	79461
170470	HA	50470	56470	79470
170471	HA	50471	56471	79471
170472	HA	50472	56472	79472
170473	HA	50473	56473	79473
170474	HA	50474	56474	79474
170475	HA	50475	56475	79475
170476	HA	50476	56476	79476
170477	HA	50477	56477	79477
170478	HA	50478	56478	79478

*170401 Sir Moir Lockhead OBE. *170405 Riverside Museum. *170407 UNIVERSITY OF ABERDEEN. *170433 Investor in People.

Class 170/5 Adtranz Turbostar

		DMSL	DMSL
170501	TS	50501	79501
170502	TS	50502	79502
170503	TS	50503	79503
170504	TS	50504	79504
170505	TS	50505	79505
170506	TS	50506	79506
170507	TS	50507	79507
170508	TS	50508	79508
170509	TS	50509	79509
170510	TS	50510	79510
170511	TS	50511	79511
170512	TS	50512	79512
170513	TS	50513	79513
170514	TS	50514	79514
170515	TS	50515	79515
170516	TS	50516	79516
170517	TS	50517	79517
170518	TS	50518	79518
170519	TS	50519	79519
170520	TS	50520	79520
170521	TS	50521	79521
170522	TS	50522	79522
170523	TS	50523	79523

Class 170/6 Adtranz Turbostar

		DMSL	MS	DMSL
170630	TS	50630	56630	79630
170631	TS	50631	56631	79631
170632	TS	50632	56632	79632
170633	TS	50633	56633	79633
170634	TS	50634	56634	79634
170635	TS	50635	56635	79635
170636	TS	50636	56636	79636
170637	TS	50637	56637	79637
170638	TS	50638	56638	79638
170639	TS	50639	56639	79639

Class 171/7 Bombardier Turbostar

		DMCL	DMSL
171721	SU	50721	79721
171722	SU	50722	79722
171723	SU	50723	79723
171724	SU	50724	79724
171725	SU	50725	79725
171726	SU	50726	79726
171727	SU	50727	79727
171728	SU	50728	79728
171729	SU	50729	79729
171730	SU	50392	79392

Class 171/8 Bombardier Turbostar

		DMCL	MS	MS	DMCL			DMCL	MS	MS	DMCL
171801	SU	50801	56801	54801	79801	171804	SU	50804	56804	54804	79804
171802	SU	50802	56802	54802	79802	171805	SU	50805	56805	54805	79805
171803	SU	50803	56803	54803	79803	171806	SU	50806	56806	54806	79806

Class 172 Bombardier Turbostar (London Overground)

		DMS	DMS			DMS	DMS
172001	WN	59311	59411	172005	WN	59315	59415
172002	WN	59312	59412	172006	WN	59316	59416
172003	WN	59313	59413	172007	WN	59317	59417
172004	WN	59314	59414	172008	WN	59318	59418

Class 172/1 Bombardier Turbostar (Chiltern Railways)

		DMS	DMS			DMSL	DMS
172101	AL	59111	59211	172103	AL	59113	59213
172102	AL	59112	59212	172104	AL	59114	59214

Class 172/2 Bombardier Turbostar (London Midland)

		DMSL	DMS			DMSL	DMSL
172211	TS	50211	79211	172217	TS	50217	79217
172212	TS	50212	79212	172218	TS	50218	79218
172213	TS	50213	79213	172219	TS	50219	79219
172214	TS	50214	79214	172220	TS	50220	79220
172215	TS	50215	79215	172221	TS	50221	79221
172216	TS	50216	79216	172222	TS	50222	79222

Class 172/3 Bombardier Turbostar (London Midland)

		DMSL	MS	DMS			DMSL	MS	DMSL
172331	TS	50331	56331	79331	172339	TS	50339	56339	79339
172332	TS	50332	56332	79332	172340	TS	50340	56340	79340
172333	TS	50333	56333	79333	172341	TS	50341	56341	79341
172334	TS	50334	56334	79334	172342	TS	50342	56342	79342
172335	TS	50335	56335	79335	172343	TS	50343	56343	79343
172336	TS	50336	56336	79336	172344	TS	50344	56344	79344
172337	TS	50337	56337	79337	172345	TS	50345	56345	79345
172338	TS	50338	56338	79338					

Class 175/0 GEC ALSTOM 'CORADIA 1000'

		DMSL	DMSL
175001	CH	50701	79701
175002	CH	50702	79702
175003	CH	50703	79703
175004	CH	50704	79704
175005	CH	50705	79705
175006	CH	50706	79706
175007	CH	50707	79707
175008	CH	50708	79708
175009	CH	50709	79709
175010	CH	50710	79710
175011	CH	50711	79711

Class 175/1 GEC ALSTOM 'CORADIA 1000'

		DMSL	MSL	DMSL
175101	CH	50751	56751	79751
175102	CH	50752	56752	79752
175103	CH	50753	56753	79753
175104	CH	50754	56754	79754
175105	CH	50755	56755	79755
175106	CH	50756	56756	79756
175107	CH	50757	56757	79757
175108	CH	50758	56758	79758
175109	CH	50759	56759	79759
175110	CH	50760	56760	79760
175111	CH	50761	56761	79761
175112	CH	50762	56762	79762
175113	CH	50763	56763	79763
175114	CH	50764	56764	79764
175115	CH	50765	56765	79765
175116	CH	50766	56766	79766

Class 180 GEC Alstom 'Adelante'

		DMSL	MFL	MSL	MSLRB	DMSL	
180101	HT	50901	54901	55901	56901	59901	
180102	OO	50902	54902	55902	56902	59902	
180103	OO	50903	54903	55903	56903	59903	
180104	OO	50904	54904	55904	56904	59904	
180105	HT	50905	54905	55905	56905	59905	THE YORKSHIRE ARTIST ASHLEY JACKSON
180106	OO	50906	54906	55906	56906	59906	
180107	HT	50907	54907	55907	56907	59907	HART OF THE NORTH
180108	OO	50908	54908	55908	56908	59908	
180109	OO	50909	54909	55909	56909	59909	
180110	OO	50910	54910	55910	56910	59910	
180111	OO	50911	54911	55911	56911	59911	
180112	HT	50912	54912	55912	56912	59912	JAMES HERRIOT
180113	OO	50913	54913	55913	56913	59913	
180114	HT	50914	54914	55914	56914	59914	

180101/105/107/112/114 in use with Grand Central. 180109/110/111/113 in use with Hull Trains.
180102/103/104/106/108 in use with First Great Western.

Class 185 Siemens Desiro U.K. 'Pennine'

		DMC	MS	DMS
185101	AK	51101	53101	54101
185102	AK	51102	53102	54102
185103	AK	51103	53103	54103
185104	AK	51104	53104	54104
185105	AK	51105	53105	54105
185106	AK	51106	53106	54106
185107	AK	51107	53107	54107
185108	AK	51108	53108	54108
185109	AK	51109	53109	54109
185110	AK	51110	53110	54110
185111	AK	51111	53111	54111
185112	AK	51112	53112	54112
185113	AK	51113	53113	54113
185114	AK	51114	53114	54114
185115	AK	51115	53115	54115
185116	AK	51116	53116	54116
185117	AK	51117	53117	54117
185118	AK	51118	53118	54118
185119	AK	51119	53119	54119
185120	AK	51120	53120	54120
185121	AK	51121	53121	54121
185122	AK	51122	53122	54122
185123	AK	51123	53123	54123
185124	AK	51124	53124	54124
185125	AK	51125	53125	54125
185126	AK	51126	53126	54126

		DMC	MS	DMS
185127	AK	51127	53127	54127
185128	AK	51128	53128	54128
185129	AK	51129	53129	54129
185130	AK	51130	53130	54130
185131	AK	51131	53131	54131
185132	AK	51132	53132	54132
185133	AK	51133	53133	54133
185134	AK	51134	53134	54134
185135	AK	51135	53135	54135
185136	AK	51136	53136	54136
185137	AK	51137	53137	54137
185138	AK	51138	53138	54138
185139	AK	51139	53139	54139
185140	AK	51140	53140	54140
185141	AK	51141	53141	54141
185142	AK	51142	53142	54142
185143	AK	51143	53143	54143
185144	AK	51144	53144	54144
185145	AK	51145	53145	54145
185146	AK	51146	53146	54146
185147	AK	51147	53147	54147
185148	AK	51148	53148	54148
185149	AK	51149	53149	54149
185150	AK	51150	53150	54150
185151	AK	51151	53151	54151

DIESEL ELECTRIC MULTIPLE UNITS

Class 201/202 (Preserved Hastings Unit) (formation operates as required)

	DMBS	TSL	TSL	TRSB	TSL	DMBS
201001SE	60000 Hastings	60501	70262	69337	60529	60118 Tunbridge Wells

Spare DMBS vehicle: 60116 Mountfield at SE

Class 220 Voyager (Bombardier)

Unit	Depot	DMS	MSRMB	MS	DMF
220001	CZ	60301	60701	60201	60401
220002	CZ	60302	60702	60202	60402
220003	CZ	60303	60703	60203	60403
220004	CZ	60304	60704	60204	60404
220005	CZ	60305	60705	60205	60405
220006	CZ	60306	60706	60206	60406
220007	CZ	60307	60707	60207	60407
220008	CZ	60308	60708	60208	60408
220009	CZ	60309	60709	60209	60409
220010	CZ	60310	60710	60210	60410
220011	CZ	60311	60711	60211	60411
220012	CZ	60312	60712	60212	60412
220013	CZ	60313	60713	60213	60413
220014	CZ	60314	60714	60214	60414
220015	CZ	60315	60715	60215	60415
220016	CZ	60316	60716	60216	60416
220017	CZ	60317	60717	60217	60417
220018	CZ	60318	60718	60218	60418
220019	CZ	60319	60719	60219	60419
220020	CZ	60320	60720	60220	60420
220021	CZ	60321	60721	60221	60421
220022	CZ	60322	60722	60222	60422
220023	CZ	60323	60723	60223	60423
220024	CZ	60324	60724	60224	60424
220025	CZ	60325	60725	60225	60425
220026	CZ	60326	60726	60226	60426
220027	CZ	60327	60727	60227	60427
220028	CZ	60328	60728	60228	60428
220029	CZ	60329	60729	60229	60429
220030	CZ	60330	60730	60230	60430
220031	CZ	60331	60731	60231	60431
220032	CZ	60332	60732	60232	60432
220033	CZ	60333	60733	60233	60433
220034	CZ	60334	60734	60234	60434

Class 221 Super Voyager (Tilting) Bombardier

Unit	Depot	DMS	MS	MS	MS	DMF	Name
221101	CZ	60351	60951	60851	60751	60451	Louis Bleriot
221102	CZ	60352	60952	60852	60752	60452	John Cabot
221103	CZ	60353	60953	60853	60753	60453	Christopher Columbus
221104	CZ	60354	60954	60854	60754	60454	Sir John Franklin
221105	CZ	60355	60955	60855	60755	60455	William Baffin
221106	CZ	60356	60956	60856	60756	60456	Willem Barents
221107	CZ	60357	60957	60857	60757	60457	Sir Martin Frobisher
221108	CZ	60358	60958	60858	60758	60458	Sir Ernest Shackleton
221109	CZ	60359	60959	60859	60759	60459	Marco Polo
221110	CZ	60360	60960	60860	60760	60460	James Cook
221111	CZ	60361	60961	60861	60761	60461	Roald Amundsen
221112	CZ	60362	60962	60862	60762	60462	Ferdinand Magellan
221113	CZ	60363	60963	60863	60763	60463	Sir Walter Raleigh
221114	CZ	60364	60964	60864	60764	60464	
221115	CZ	60365	60965	60865	60765	60465	Polmadie Depot
221116	CZ	60366	60966	60866	60766	60466	
221117	CZ	60367	60967	60867	60767	60467	
221118	CZ	60368	60968	60868	60768	60468	
221119	CZ	60369	60769	60969	60869	60469	
221120	CZ	60370	60770	60970	60870	60470	
221121	CZ	60371	60771	60971	60871	60471	
221122	CZ	60372	60772	60972	60872	60472	
221123	CZ	60373	60773	60973	60873	60473	

221124	CZ	60374	60774	60974	60874	60474	
221125	CZ	60375	60775	60975	60875	60475	
221126	CZ	60376	60776	60976	60876	60476	
221127	CZ	60377	60777	60977	60877	60477	
221128	CZ	60378	60778	60978	60878	60478	
221129	CZ	60379	60779	60979	60879	60479	
221130	CZ	60380	60780	60980	60880	60480	
221131	CZ	60381	60781	60981	60881	60481	
221132	CZ	60382	60782	60982	60882	60482	
221133	CZ	60383	60783	60983	60883	60483	
221134	CZ	60384	60784	60984	60884	60484	
221135	CZ	60385	60785	60985	60885	60485	
221136	CZ	60386	60786	60986	60886	60486	
221137	CZ	60387	60787	60987	60887	60487	
221138	CZ	60388	60788	60988	60888	60488	
221139	CZ	60389	60789	60989	60889	60489	
221140	CZ	60390	60790	60990	60890	60490	
221141	CZ	60391	60791	60991		60491	
221142	CZ	60392	60992	60994	60792	60492	BOMBARDIER Voyager
221143	CZ	60393	60993	60794	60793	60493	Auguste Picard
221144	CZs	60394				60494	

Class 222 East Midlands Mainline Meridian (Bombardier)

		DMS	MS	MS	MSRMB	MF	MF	DMF	
222001	DY	60161	60551	60561	60621	60341	60445	60241	THE ENTREPRENEUR EXPRESS
222002	DY	60162	60544	60562	60622	60342	60346	60242	THE CUTLERS COMPANY
222003	DY	60163*	60553	60563	60623	60343	60446	60243	*TORNADO
222004	DY	60164	60554	60564	60624	60344	60345	60244	
222005	DY	60165	60555	60565	60625	60443	60347	60245	
222006	DY	60166	60556	60566	60626	60441	60447	60246	THE CARBON CUTTER
		DMS	**MS**	**MSRMB**	**MC**	**DMF**			
222007	DY	60167	60567	60627	60442	60247			
222008	DY	60168	60545	60628	60918	60248			
222009	DY	60169	60557	60629	60919	60249			
222010	DY	60170	60546	60630	60920	60250			
222011	DY	60171	60531	60631	60921	60251			
222012	DY	60172	60532	60632	60922	60252			
222013	DY	60173	60533	60633	60923	60253			
222014	DY	60174	60534	60634	60924	60254			
222015	DY	60175	60535	60635	60925	60255			
222016	DY	60176	60536	60636	60926	60256			
222017	DY	60177	60537	60637	60927	60257			
222018	DY	60178	60444	60638	60928	60258			
222019	DY	60179	60547	60639	60929	60259			
222020	DY	60180	60543	60640	60930	60260			

222021	DY	60181	60552	60641	60931	60261	
222022	DY	60182	60542	60642	60932	60262	INVEST IN NOTTINGHAM
222023	DY	60183	60541	60643	60933	60263	

Class 222/1 Hull Trains (Bombardier)

		DMS	MSRMB	MC	DMF			DMS	MSRMB	MC	DMF
222101	DY	60191	60681	60571	60271	222103	DY	60193	60683	60573	60273
222102	DY	60192	60682	60572	60272	222104	DY	60194	60684	60574	60274

ELECTRIC MULTIPLE UNITS

Class 313 BREL York (Inner Suburban)

		DMSO	PTSO	BDMSO			DMSO	PTSO	BDMSO
313018	HE	62546	71230	62610	313047	HE	62575	71259	62639
313024	HE	62552	71236	62616	313048	HE	62576	71260	62640
313025	HE	62553	71237	62617	313049	HE	62577	71261	62641
313026	HE	62554	71238	62618	313050	HE	62578	71262	62649
313027	HE	62555	71239	62619	313051	HE	62579	71263	62624
313028	HE	62556	71240	62620	313052	HE	62580	71264	62644
313029	HE	62557	71241	62621	313053	HE	62581	71265	62645
313030	HE	62558	71242	62622	313054	HE	62582	71266	62646
313031	HE	62559	71243	62623	313055	HE	62583	71267	62647
313032	HE	62560	71244	62643	313056	HE	62584	71268	62648
313033	HE	62561	71245	62625	313057	HE	62585	71269	62642
313035	HE	62563	71247	62627	313058	HE	62586	71270	62650
313036	HE	62564	71248	62628	313059	HE	62587	71271	62651
313037	HE	62565	71249	62629	313060	HE	62588	71272	62652
313038	HE	62566	71250	62630	313061	HE	62589	71273	62653
313039	HE	62567	71251	62631	313062	HE	62590	71274	62654
313040	HE	62568	71252	62632	313063	HE	62591	71275	62655
313041	HE	62569	71253	62633	313064	HE	62592	71276	62656
313042	HE	62570	71254	62634					
313043	HE	62571	71255	62635	313121	WB	62549	71233	62613
313044	HE	62572	71256	62636	313122	HE	62550	71234	62614
313045	HE	62573	71257	62637	313123	HE	62551	71235	62615
313046	HE	62574	71258	62638	313134	HE	62562	71246	62626

313054 Captain William Leefe Robinson V.C. 313134 City of London.

Class 313/2 BREL York

		DMSO	TSO	BDMSO			DMSO	TSO	BDMSO
313201	BI	62529	71213	62593	313211	BI	62539	71223	62603
313202	BI	62530	71214	62594	313212	BI	62540	71224	62604
313203	BI	62531	71215	62595	313213	BI	62541	71225	62605
313204	BI	62532	71216	62596	313214	BI	62542	71226	62606
313205	BI	62533	71217	62597	313215	BI	62543	71227	62607
313206	BI	62534	71218	62598	313216	BI	62544	71228	62608
313207	BI	62535	71219	62599	313217	BI	62545	71229	62609
313208	BI	62536	71220	62600	313219	BI	62547	71231	62611
313209	BI	62537	71221	62601	313220	BI	62548	71232	62612
313210	BI	62538	71222	62602					

Refurbished and renumbered from 313101-313120

Class 314 BREL York (Inner Suburban)

		DMSO	PTSO	DMSO			DMSO	PTSO	DMSO
314201	GW	64583	71450	64584	314209	GW	64599	71458	64600
314202	GW	64585	71451	64586	314210	GW	64601	71459	64602
314203	GW	64587	71452	64588	314211	GW	64603	71460	64604
314204	GW	64589	71453	64590	314212	GW	64605	71461	64606
314205	GW	64591	71454	64592	314213	GW	64607	71462	64608
314206	GW	64593	71455	64594	314214	GW	64609	71463	64610
314207	GW	64595	71456	64596	314215	GW	64611	71464	64612
314208	GW	64597	71457	64598	314216	GW	64613	71465	64614

Class 315 BREL York (Inner Suburban)

		DMSO	TSO	PTSO	DMSO			DMSO	TSO	PTSO	DMSO
315801	IL	64461	71281	71389	64462	315815	IL	64489	71295	71403	64490
315802	IL	64463	71282	71390	64464	315816	IL	64491	71296	71404	64492
315803	IL	64465	71283	71391	64466	315817	IL	64493	71297	71405	64494
315804	IL	64467	71284	71392	64468	315818	IL	64495	71298	71406	64496
315805	IL	64469	71285	71393	64470	315819	IL	64497	71299	71407	64498
315806	IL	64471	71286	71394	64472	315820	IL	64499	71300	71408	64500
315807	IL	64473	71287	71395	64474	315821	IL	64501	71301	71409	64502
315808	IL	64475	71288	71396	64476	315822	IL	64503	71302	71410	64504
315809	IL	64477	71289	71397	64478	315823	IL	64505	71303	71411	64506
315810	IL	64479	71290	71398	64480	315824	IL	64507	71304	71412	64508
315811	IL	64481	71291	71399	64482	315825	IL	64509	71305	71413	64510
315812	IL	64483	71292	71400	64484	315826	IL	64511	71306	71414	64512
315813	IL	64485	71293	71401	64486	315827	IL	64513	71307	71415	64514
315814	IL	64487	71294	71402	64488	315828	IL	64515	71308	71416	64516

315829	IL	64517	71309	71417	64518	315846	IL	64551	71326	71434	64552
315830	IL	64519	71310	71418	64520	315847	IL	64553	71327	71435	64554
315831	IL	64521	71311	71419	64522	315848	IL	64555	71328	71436	64556
315832	IL	64523	71312	71420	64524	315849	IL	64557	71329	71437	64558
315833	IL	64525	71313	71421	64526	315850	IL	64559	71330	71438	64560
315834	IL	64527	71314	71422	64528	315851	IL	64561	71331	71439	64562
315835	IL	64529	71315	71423	64530	315852	IL	64563	71332	71440	64564
315836	IL	64531	71316	71424	64532	315853	IL	64565	71333	71441	64566
315837	IL	64533	71317	71425	64534	315854	IL	64567	71334	71442	64568
315838	IL	64535	71318	71426	64536	315855	IL	64569	71335	71443	64570
315839	IL	64537	71319	71427	64538	315856	IL	64571	71336	71444	64572
315840	IL	64539	71320	71428	64540	315857	IL	64573	71337	71445	64574
315841	IL	64541	71321	71429	64542	315858	IL	64575	71338	71446	64576
315842	IL	64543	71322	71430	64544	315859	IL	64577	71339	71447	64578
315843	IL	64545	71323	71431	64546	315860	IL	64575	71340	71448	64576
315844	IL	64547	71324	71432	64548	315861	IL	64581	71341	71449	64582
315845	IL	64549	71325	71433	64550						

315817 Transport for London. 315829 London Borough of Havering, Celebrating 40 years.
315845 Herbie Woodward. 315857 Stratford Connections.

Class 317/1 BREL York/Derby

		DTSO	MSO	TCO	DTSO			DTSO	MSO	TCO	DTSO
317337	HE	77036	62671	71613	77084	317343	HE	77042	62703	71619	77090
317338	HE	77037	62698	71614	77085	317344	HE	77029	62690	71620	77091
317339	HE	77038	62699	71615	77086	317345	HE	77044	62705	71621	77092
317340	HE	77039	62700	71616	77087	317346	HE	77045	62706	71622	77093
317341	HE	77040	62701	71617	77088	317347	HE	77046	62707	71623	77094
317342	HE	77041	62702	71618	77089	317348	HE	77047	62708	71624	77095

317345 Driver John Webb. 317348 Richard A Jenner.

Class 317/5 Renumbered from 317301-317307/311-313/315-318/320

		DTSO	MSO	TCO	DTSO			DTSO	MSO	TCO	DTSO
317501	IL	77024	62661	71577	77048	317509	IL	77011	62672	71588	77059
317502	IL	77001	62662	71578	77049	317510	IL	77012	62673	71589	77060
317503	IL	77002	62663	71579	77050	317511	IL	77014	62675	71591	77062
317504	IL	77003	62664	71580	77051	317512	IL	77015	62676	71592	77063
317505	IL	77004	62665	71581	77052	317513	IL	77016	62677	71593	77064
317506	IL	77005	62666	71582	77053	317514	IL	77017	62678	71594	77065
317507	IL	77006	62667	71583	77054	317515	IL	77019	62680	71596	77067
317508	IL	77010	62697	71587	77058						

317507 University of Cambridge 800 years 1209-2009.

Class 317/6 Refurbished

		DTSO	MSO	TSO	DTCO			DTSO	MSO	TSO	DTCO
317649	IL	77200	62846	71734	77220	317661	IL	77212	62858	71746	77232
317650	IL	77201	62847	71735	77221	317662	IL	77213	62859	71747	77233
317651	IL	77202	62848	71736	77222	317663	IL	77214	62860	71748	77234
317652	IL	77203	62849	71739	77223	317664	IL	77215	62861	71749	77235
317653	IL	77204	62850	71738	77224	317665	IL	77216	62862	71750	77236
317654	IL	77205	62851	71737	77225	317666	IL	77217	62863	71752	77237
317655	IL	77206	62852	71740	77226	317667	IL	77218	62864	71751	77238
317656	IL	77207	62853	71742	77227	317668	IL	77219	62865	71753	77239
317657	IL	77208	62854	71741	77228	317669	IL	77280	62886	71762	77284
317658	IL	77209	62855	71743	77229	317670	IL	77281	62887	71763	77285
317659	IL	77210	62856	71744	77230	317671	IL	77282	62888	71764	77286
317660	IL	77211	62857	71745	77231	317672	IL	77283	62889	71765	77287

317654 Richard Wells.

Class 317/7 Refurbished at Wolverton (Stansted Express)

		DTSO	MSO	TSO	DTCO			DTSO	MSO	TSO	DTCO
317708	ZG	77007	62668	71584	77055	317722	ILs	77021	62682	71598	77069
317709	ZG	77008	62669	71585	77056	317723	ZG	77022	62683	71599	77070
317710	ZG	77009	62670	71586	77057	317729	ZG	77028	62689	71605	77076
317714	ZG	77013	62674	71590	77061	317732	ZG	77031	62692	71608	77079
317719	ZG	77018	62679	71595	77066						

317709 Len Camp. 317723 The Tottenham Flyer.

Class 317/8 Refurbished by Wabtec for Stanstead Express

		DTSO	MSO	TCO	DTSO			DTSO	MSO	TCO	DTSO
317881	IL	77020	62681	71597	77068	317887	IL	77043	62704	71606	77077
317882	IL	77023	62684	71600	77071	317888	IL	77030	62691	71607	77078
317883	IL	77000	62685	71601	77072	317889	IL	77032	62693	71609	77080
317884	IL	77025	62686	71602	77073	317890	IL	77033	62694	71610	77081
317885	IL	77026	62687	71603	77074	317891	IL	77034	62695	71611	77082
317886	IL	77027	62688	71604	77075	317892	IL	77035	62696	71612	77083

renumbered from 317321/324/325/326/327/328/330/331/333/334/335/336

317892 Ilford Depot.

Class 318 BREL York

		DTSO	MSO	DTSO
318250	GW	77260	62866	77240
318251	GW	77261	62867	77241
318252	GW	77262	62868	77242
318253	GW	77263	62869	77243
318254	GW	77264	62870	77244
318255	GW	77265	62871	77245
318256	GW	77266	62872	77246
318257	GW	77267	62873	77247
318258	GW	77268	62874	77248
318259	GW	77269	62875	77249
318260	GW	77270	62876	77250
318261	GW	77271	62877	77251
318262	GW	77272	62878	77252
318263	GW	77273	62879	77253
318264	GW	77274	62880	77254
318265	GW	77275	62881	77255
318266	GW	77276	62882	77256
318267	GW	77277	62883	77257
318268	GW	77278	62884	77258
318269	GW	77279	62885	77259
318270	GW	77289	62890	77288

318250 GEOFF SHAW. 318259 Citizens' Network. 318266 Strathclyder.

Class 319/0 BREL York

		DTSO	MSO	TSO	DTSO
319001	BF	77291	62891	71772	77290
319002	BF	77293	62892	71773	77292
319003	BF	77295	62893	71774	77294
319004	BF	77297	62894	71775	77296
319005	BF	77299	62895	71776	77298
319006	BF	77301	62896	71777	77300
319007	BF	77303	62897	71778	77302
319008	BF	77305	62898	71779	77304
319009	BF	77307	62899	71780	77306
319010	BF	77309	62900	71781	77308
319011	BF	77311	62901	71782	77310
319012	BF	77313	62902	71783	77312
319013	BF	77315	62903	71784	77314

319008 Cheriton. 319009 Coquelles. 319011 John Ruskin College. 319013 The Surrey Hills.

Class 319/2

		DTSO	MSO	TSO	DTCO
319214	BF	77317	62904	71785	77316
319215	BF	77319	62905	71786	77318
319216	BF	77321	62906	71787	77320
319217	BF	77323	62907	71788	77322
319218	BF	77325	62908	71789	77324
319219	BF	77327	62909	71790	77326
319220	BF	77329	62910	71791	77328

319217 Brighton. 319218 Croydon.

Class 319/3

		DTSO	MSO	TSO	DTSO
319361	BF	77459	63043	71929	77458
319362	BF	77461	63044	71930	77460
319363	BF	77463	63045	71931	77462
319364	BF	77465	63046	71932	77464

319365	BF	77467	63047	71933	77466	319376	BF	77489	63058	71944	77488
319366	BF	77469	63048	71934	77468	319377	BF	77491	63059	71945	77490
319367	BF	77471	63049	71935	77470	319378	BF	77493	63060	71946	77492
319368	BF	77473	63050	71936	77472	319379	BF	77495	63061	71947	77494
319369	BF	77475	63051	71937	77474	319380	BF	77497	63062	71948	77496
319370	BF	77477	63052	71938	77476	319381	BF	77973	63093	71979	77974
319371	BF	77479	63053	71939	77478	319382	BF	77975	63094	71980	77976
319372	BF	77481	63054	71940	77480	319383	BF	77977	63095	71981	77978
319373	BF	77483	63055	71941	77482	319384	BF	77979	63096	71982	77980
319374	BF	77485	63056	71942	77484	319385	BF	77981	63097	71983	77982
319375	BF	77487	63057	71943	77486	319386	BF	77983	63098	71984	77984

319364 Transforming Farringdon. 319365 Transforming Blackfriars. 319374 Bedford Cauldwell TMD.

Class 319/4 (converted from 319/0)

		DTCO	MSO	TSO	DTSO			DTCO	MSO	TSO	DTSO
319421	BF	77331	62911	71792	77330	319441	BF	77371	62931	71812	77370
319422	BF	77333	62912	71793	77332	319442	BF	77373	62932	71813	77372
319423	BF	77335	62913	71794	77334	319443	BF	77375	62933	71814	77374
319424	BF	77337	62914	71795	77336	319444	BF	77377	62934	71815	77376
319425	BF	77339	62915	71796	77338	319445	BF	77379	62935	71816	77378
319426	BF	77341	62916	71797	77340	319446	BF	77381	62936	71817	77380
319427	BF	77343	62917	71798	77342	319447	BF	77431	62961	71866	77430
319428	BF	77345	62918	71799	77344	319448	BF	77357	62962	71867	77432
319429	BF	77347	62919	71800	77346	319449	BF	77435	62963	71868	77434
319430	BF	77349	62920	71801	77348	319450	BF	77437	62964	71869	77436
319431	BF	77351	62921	71802	77350	319451	BF	77439	62965	71870	77438
319432	BF	77353	62922	71803	77352	319452	BF	77441	62966	71871	77440
319433	BF	77355	62923	71804	77354	319453	BF	77443	62967	71872	77442
319434	BF	77433	62924	71805	77356	319454	BF	77445	62968	71873	77444
319435	BF	77359	62925	71806	77358	319455	BF	77447	62969	71874	77446
319436	BF	77361	62926	71807	77360	319456	BF	77449	62970	71875	77448
319437	BF	77363	62927	71808	77362	319457	BF	77451	62971	71876	77450
319438	BF	77365	62928	71809	77364	319458	BF	77453	62972	71877	77452
319439	BF	77367	62929	71810	77366	319459	BF	77455	62973	71878	77454
319440	BF	77369	62930	71811	77368	319460	BF	77457	62974	71879	77456

319425 Transforming Travel - First Capital Connect.
319435 Adrian Jackson-Robbins, Chairman 1987-2007 Association of Public Transport Users. 319441 Driver Mick Winnett.
319446 St Pancras International. 319448 Elstree Studios. 319449 King's Cross Thameslink.

Class 320 BREL York (Suburban)

		DTSO	MSO	DTSO
320301	GW	77899	63021	77921
320302	GW	77900	63022	77922
320303	GW	77901	63023	77923
320304	GW	77902	63024	77924
320305	GW	77903	63025	77925
320306	GW	77904	63026	77926
320307	GW	77905	63027	77927
320308	GW	77906	63028	77928
320309	GW	77907	63029	77929
320310	GW	77908	63030	77930
320311	GW	77909	63031	77931
320312	GW	77910	63032	77932
320313	GW	77911	63033	77933
320314	GW	77912	63034	77934
320315	GW	77913	63035	77935
320316	GW	77914	63036	77936
320317	GW	77915	63037	77937
320318	GW	77916	63038	77938
320319	GW	77917	63039	77939
320320	GW	77918	63040	77940
320321	GW	77919	63041	77941
320322	GW	77920	63042	77942

320305 GLASGOW SCHOOL of ART 1844-150-1994. 320309 Radio Clyde 25th Anniversary.
320312 Sir William A Smith, Founder of the Boys Brigade.

Class 321/3 BREL York

		DTCO	MSO	TSO	DTSO
321301	IL	78049	62975	71880	77853
321302	IL	78050	62976	71881	77854
321303	IL	78051	62977	71882	77855
321304	IL	78052	62978	71883	77856
321305	IL	78053	62979	71884	77857
321306	IL	78054	62980	71885	77858
321307	IL	78055	62981	71886	77859
321308	IL	78056	62982	71887	77860
321309	IL	78057	62983	71888	77861
321310	IL	78058	62984	71889	77862
321311	IL	78059	62985	71890	77863
321312	IL	78060	62986	71891	77864
321313	IL	78061	62987	71892	77865
321314	IL	78062	62988	71893	77866
321315	IL	78063	62989	71894	77867
321316	IL	78064	62990	71895	77868
321317	IL	78065	62991	71896	77869
321318	IL	78066	62992	71897	77870
321319	IL	78067	62993	71898	77871
321320	IL	78068	62994	71899	77872
321321	IL	78069	62995	71900	77873
321322	IL	78070	62996	71901	77874
321323	IL	78071	62997	71902	77875
321324	IL	78072	62998	71903	77876
321325	IL	78073	62999	71904	77877
321326	IL	78074	63000	71905	77878
321327	IL	78075	63001	71906	77879
321328	IL	78076	63002	71907	77880
321329	IL	78077	63003	71908	77881
321330	IL	78078	63004	71909	77882
321331	IL	78079	63005	71910	77883
321332	IL	78080	63006	71911	77884
321333	IL	78081	63007	71912	77885
321334	IL	78082	63008	71913	77886
321335	IL	78083	63009	71914	77887
321336	IL	78084	63010	71915	77888
321337	IL	78085	60311	71916	77889
321338	IL	78086	63012	71917	77890
321339	IL	78087	63013	71918	77891
321340	IL	78088	63014	71919	77892
321341	IL	78089	63015	71920	77893
321342	IL	78090	63016	71921	77894
321343	IL	78091	63017	71922	77895
321344	IL	78092	63018	71923	77896
321345	IL	78093	63019	71924	77897
321346	IL	78094	63020	71925	77898
321347	IL	78131	63105	71991	78280
321348	IL	78132	63106	71992	78281
321349	IL	78133	63107	71993	78282
321350	IL	78134	63108	71994	78283

321351	IL	78135	63109	71995	78284	321359	IL	78143	63117	72003	78292
321352	IL	78136	63110	71996	78285	321360	IL	78144	63118	72004	78293
321353	IL	78137	63111	71997	78286	321361	IL	78145	63119	72005	78294
321354	IL	78138	63112	71998	78287	321362	IL	78146	63120	72006	78295
321355	IL	78139	63113	71999	78288	321363	IL	78147	63121	72007	78296
321356	IL	78140	63114	72000	78289	321364	IL	78148	63122	72008	78297
321357	IL	78141	63115	72001	78290	321365	IL	78149	63123	72009	78298
321358	IL	78142	63116	72002	78291	321366	IL	78150	63124	72010	78299

321312 Southend-on-Sea. 321313 University of Essex. 321321 NSPCC ESSEX FULL STOP. 321334 Amsterdam. 321336 GEOFFREY FREEMAN ALLEN. 321342 R.Barnes.
321343 RSA RAILWAY STUDY ASSOCIATION. 321351 London Southend Airport. 321361 Phoenix.

Class 321/4

		DTCO	MSO	TSO	DTSO			DTCO	MSO	TSO	DTSO
321401	HE	78095	63063	71949	77943	321425	IL	78119	63087	71973	77967
321402	HE	78096	63064	71950	77944	321426	IL	78120	63088	71974	77968
321403	HE	78097	63065	71951	77945	321427	IL	78121	63089	71975	77969
321404	HE	78098	63066	71952	77946	321428	IL	78122	63090	71976	77970
321405	HE	78099	63067	71953	77947	321429	IL	78123	63091	71977	77971
321406	HE	78100	63068	71954	77948	321430	IL	78124	63092	71978	77972
321407	HE	78101	63069	71955	77949	321431	IL	78151	63125	72011	78300
321408	HE	78102	63070	71956	77950	321432	IL	78152	63126	72012	78301
321409	HE	78103	63071	71957	77951	321433	IL	78153	63127	72013	78302
321410	HE	78104	63072	71958	77952	321434	IL	78154	63128	72014	78303
321411	NN	78105	63073	71959	77953	321435	IL	78155	63129	72015	78304
321412	NN	78106	63074	71960	77954	321436	IL	78156	63130	72016	78305
321413	NN	78107	63075	71961	77955	321437	IL	78157	63131	72017	78306
321414	NN	78108	63076	71962	77956	321438	IL	78158	63132	72018	78307
321415	NN	78109	63077	71963	77957	321439	IL	78159	63133	72019	78309
321416	NN	78110	63078	71964	77958	321440	IL	78160	63134	72020	78310
321417	NN	78111	63079	71965	77959	321441	IL	78161	63135	72021	78311
321418	HE	78112	63080	71968	77962	321442	IL	78162	63136	72022	78312
321419	HE	78113	63081	71967	77961	321443	IL	78125	63099	71985	78274
321420	HE	78114	63082	71966	77960	321444	IL	78126	63100	71986	78275
321421	IL	78115	63083	71969	77963	321445	IL	78127	63101	71987	78276
321422	IL	78116	63084	71970	77964	321446	IL	78128	63102	71988	78277
321423	IL	78117	63085	71971	77965	321447	IL	78129	63103	71989	78278
321424	IL	78118	63086	71972	77966	321448	IL	78130	63104	71990	78279

321403 Stewart Fleming Signalman King's Cross. 321428 The Essex Commuter. 321444 Essex Lifeboats.
321446 George Mullings.

Class 321/9

		DTSO	MSO	TSO	DTSO
321901	NL	77990	63153	72128	77993
321902	NL	77991	63154	72129	77994
321903	NL	77992	63155	72130	77995

Class 322 BREL York (Northern)

		DTCO	MSO	TSO	DTSO
322481	NL	78163	63137	72023	77985
322482	NL	78164	63138	72024	77986
322483	NL	78165	63139	72025	77987
322484	NL	78166	63140	72026	77988
322485	NL	78167	63141	72027	77989

Class 323/0 Hunslet Transportation Projects (Suburban)

		DMSO	PTSO	DMSO
323201	SO	64001	72201	65001
323202	SO	64002	72202	65002
323203	SO	64003	72203	65003
323204	SO	64004	72204	65004
323205	SO	64005	72205	65005
323206	SO	64006	72206	65006
323207	SO	64007	72207	65007
323208	SO	64008	72208	65008
323209	SO	64009	72209	65009
323210	SO	64010	72210	65010
323211	SO	64011	72211	65011
323212	SO	64012	72212	65012
323213	SO	64013	72213	65013
323214	SO	64014	72214	65014
323215	SO	64015	72215	65015
323216	SO	64016	72216	65016
323217	SO	64017	72217	65017
323218	SO	64018	72218	65018
323219	SO	64019	72219	65019
323220	SO	64020	72220	65020
323221	SO	64021	72221	65021
323222	SO	64022	72222	65022
323223	MA	64023	72223	65023
323224	MA	64024	72224	65024
323225	MA	64025	72225	65025
323226	MA	64026	72226	65026
323227	MA	64027	72227	65027
323228	MA	64028	72228	65028
323229	MA	64029	72229	65029
323230	MA	64030	72230	65030
323231	MA	64031	72231	65031
323232	MA	64032	72232	65032
323233	MA	64033	72233	65033
323234	MA	64034	72234	65034
323235	MA	64035	72235	65035
323236	MA	64036	72236	65036
323237	MA	64037	72237	65037
323238	MA	64038	72238	65038
323239	MA	64039	72239	65039
323240	SO	64040	72340	65040
323241	SO	64041	72341	65041
323242	SO	64042	72342	65042
323243	SO	64043	72343	65043

CLASS 325 ABB Derby Royal Mail Unit (dual voltage)

		DTPMV	MPMV	TPMV	DTPMV
325001	CE	68300	68340	68360	68301
325002	CE	68302	68341	68361	68303
325003	CE	68304	68342	68362	68305
325004	CE	68306	68343	68363	68307
325005	CE	68308	68344	68364	68309
325006	CE	68310	68345	68365	68311
325007	CE	68312	68346	68366	68313
325008	CE	68314	68347	68367	68315
325009	CE	68316	68349	68368	68317
325011	CE	68320	68350	68370	68321
325012	CE	68322	68351	68371	68323
325013	CE	68324	68352	68372	68325
325014	CE	68326	68353	68373	68327
325015	CE	68328	68354	68374	68329
325016	CE	68330	68355	68375	68331

325002 Royal Mail North Wales & North West. 325006 John Grierson. 325008 Peter Howarth CBE.

CLASS 332 Siemens (HEATHROW EXPRESS)

		DMFO	TSO	PTSO	TSO	DMSO
332001	OH	78400	72412	63400		78401
332002	OH	78402	72409	63401		78403
332003	OH	78404	72407	63402		78405
332004	OH	78406	72405	63403		78407
332005	OH	78408	72411	63404	72417	78409
332006	OH	78410	72410	63405	72415	78411
332007	OH	78412	72401	63406	72414	78413
332008	OH	78414	72413	63407	72418	78415
332009	OH	78416	72400	63408	72416	78417
332010	OH	78418	72402	63409		78419
332011	OH	78420	72403	63410		78421
332012	OH	78422	72404	63411		78423
332013	OH	78424	72408	63412		78425
332014	OH	78426	72406	63413		78427

Class 333 Siemens (Suburban)

		DMSO	PTSO	TSO	DMSO
333001	NL	78451	74461	74477	78452
333002	NL	78453	74462	74478	78454
333003	NL	78455	74463	74479	78456
333004	NL	78457	74464	74480	78458
333005	NL	78459	74465	74481	78460
333006	NL	78461	74466	74482	78462
333007	NL	78463	74467	74483	78464
333008	NL	78465	74468	74484	78466
333009	NL	78467	74469	74485	78468
333010	NL	78469	74470	74486	78470
333011	NL	78471	74471	74487	78472
333012	NL	78473	74472	74488	78474
333013	NL	78475	74473	74489	78476
333014	NL	78477	74474	74490	78478
333015	NL	78479	74475	74491	78480
333016	NL	78481	74476	74492	78482

333007 Alderman J Arthur Godwin, First Lord Mayor of Bradford 1907.

Class 334 ALSTOM JUNIPER (Suburban)

		DMSO	PTSO	DMSO
334001	GW	64101	74301	65101
334002	GW	64102	74302	65102
334003	GW	64103	74303	65103
334004	GW	64104	74304	65104
334005	GW	64105	74305	65105
334006	GW	64106	74306	65106
334007	GW	64107	74307	65107
334008	GW	64108	74308	65108
334009	GW	64109	74309	65109
334010	GW	64110	74310	65110
334011	GW	64111	74311	65111
334012	GW	64112	74312	65112
334013	GW	64113	74313	65113
334014	GW	64114	74314	65114
334015	GW	64115	74315	65115
334016	GW	64116	74316	65116
334017	GW	64117	74317	65117
334018	GW	64118	74318	65118
334019	GW	64119	74319	65119
334020	GW	64120	74320	65120
334021	GW	64121	74321	65121
334022	GW	64122	74322	65122
334023	GW	64123	74323	65123
334024	GW	64124	74324	65124
334025	GW	64125	74325	65125
334026	GW	64126	74326	65126
334027	GW	64127	74327	65127
334028	GW	64128	74328	65128
334029	GW	64129	74329	65129
334030	GW	64130	74330	65130
334031	GW	64131	74331	65131
334032	GW	64132	74332	65132
334033	GW	64133	74333	65133
334034	GW	64134	74334	65134
334035	GW	64135	74335	65135
334036	GW	64136	74336	65136
334037	GW	64137	74337	65137
334038	GW	64138	74338	65138
334039	GW	64139	74339	65139
334040	GW	64140	74340	65140

334001 Donald Dewer. 334021 Larkhall.

Class 350/1 Siemens Desiro UK

		DMCO	TCO	PTSO	DMCO
350101	NN	63711	66861	66811	63761
350102	NN	63712	66862	66812	63762
350103	NN	63713	66863	66813	63765
350104	NN	63714	66864	66814	63764
350105	NN	63715	66868	66815	63763
350106	NN	63716	66866	66816	63766
350107	NN	63717	66867	66817	63767
350108	NN	63718	66865	66818	63768
350109	NN	63719	66869	66819	63769
350110	NN	63720	66870	66820	63770
350111	NN	63721	66871	66821	63771
350112	NN	63722	66872	66822	63772
350113	NN	63723	66873	66823	63773
350114	NN	63724	66874	66824	63774
350115	NN	63725	66875	66825	63775
350116	NN	63726	66876	66826	63776
350117	NN	63727	66877	66827	63777
350118	NN	63728	66878	66828	63778
350119	NN	63729	66879	66829	63779
350120	NN	63730	66880	66830	63780
350121	NN	63731	66881	66831	63781
350122	NN	63732	66882	66832	63782
350123	NN	63733	66883	66833	63783
350124	NN	63734	66884	66834	63784
350125	NN	63735	66885	66835	63785
350126	NN	63736	66886	66836	63786
350127	NN	63737	66887	66837	63787
350128	NN	63738	66888	66838	63788
350129	NN	63739	66889	66839	63789
350130	NN	63740	66890	66840	63790

Class 350/2 Siemens Desiro UK

		DMSO	TCO	PTSO	DMSO			DMSO	TCO	PTSO	DMSO
350231	NN	61431	65231	67531	61531	350250	NN	61450	65250	67550	61550
350232	NN	61432	65232	67532	61532	350251	NN	61451	65251	67551	61551
350233	NN	61433	65233	67533	61533	350252	NN	61452	65252	67552	61552
350234	NN	61434	65234	67534	61534	350253	NN	61453	65253	67553	61553
350235	NN	61435	65235	67535	61535	350254	NN	61454	65254	67554	61554
350236	NN	61436	65236	67536	61536	350255	NN	61455	65255	67555	61555
350237	NN	61437	65237	67537	61537	350256	NN	61456	65256	67556	61556
350238	NN	61438	65238	67538	61538	350257	NN	61457	65257	67557	61557
350239	NN	61439	65239	67539	61539	350258	NN	61458	65258	67558	61558
350240	NN	61440	65240	67540	61540	350259	NN	61459	65259	67559	61559
350241	NN	61441	65241	67541	61541	350260	NN	61460	65260	67560	61560
350242	NN	61442	65242	67542	61542	350261	NN	61461	65261	67561	61561
350243	NN	61443	65243	67543	61543	350262	NN	61462	65262	67562	61562
350244	NN	61444	65244	67544	61544	350263	NN	61463	65263	67563	61563
350245	NN	61445	65245	67545	61545	350264	NN	61464	65264	67564	61564
350246	NN	61446	65246	67546	61546	350265	NN	61465	65265	67565	61565
350247	NN	61447	65247	67547	61547	350266	NN	61466	65266	67566	61566
350248	NN	61448	65248	67548	61548	350267	NN	61467	65267	67567	61567
350249	NN	61449	65249	67549	61549						

350232 Chad Varah.

Class 350/3 Siemens 10 on order for London Midland due 2014

	DMSO	TCO	PTSO	DMSO		DMSO	TCO	PTSO	DMSO
3503xx					3503xx				
3503xx					3503xx				
3503xx					3503xx				
3503xx					3503xx				
3503xx					3503xx				

350/4 Siemens 10 on order for First TransPennine, due late 2013

	DMSO	TCO	PTSO	DMSO		DMSO	TCO	PTSO	DMSO
3504xx					3504xx				
3504xx					3504xx				
3504xx					3504xx				
3504xx					3504xx				
3504xx					3504xx				

Class 357 Adtranz/Bombardier Derby Electrostar (Outer Suburban)

		DMSO	MSO	PTSO	DMSO
357001	EM	67651	74151	74051	67751
357002	EM	67652	74152	74052	67752
357003	EM	67653	74153	74053	67753
357004	EM	67654	74154	74054	67754
357005	EM	67655	74155	74055	67755
357006	EM	67656	74156	74056	67756
357007	EM	67657	74157	74057	67757
357008	EM	67658	74158	74058	67758
357009	EM	67659	74159	74059	67759
357010	EM	67660	74160	74060	67760
357011	EM	67661	74161	74061	67761
357012	EM	67662	74162	74062	67762
357013	EM	67663	74163	74063	67763
357014	EM	67664	74164	74064	67764
357015	EM	67665	74165	74065	67765
357016	EM	67666	74166	74066	67766
357017	EM	67667	74167	74067	67767
357018	EM	67668	74168	74068	67768
357019	EM	67669	74169	74069	67769
357020	EM	67670	74170	74070	67770
357021	EM	67671	74171	74071	67771
357022	EM	67672	74172	74072	67772
357023	EM	67673	74173	74073	67773
357024	EM	67674	74174	74074	67774
357025	EM	67675	74175	74075	67775
357026	EM	67676	74176	74076	67776
357027	EM	67677	74177	74077	67777
357028	EM	67678	74178	74078	67778
357029	EM	67679	74179	74079	67779
357030	EM	67680	74180	74080	67780
357031	EM	67681	74181	74081	67781
357032	EM	67682	74182	74082	67782
357033	EM	67683	74183	74083	67783
357034	EM	67684	74184	74084	67784
357035	EM	67685	74185	74085	67785
357036	EM	67686	74186	74086	67786
357037	EM	67687	74187	74087	67787
357038	EM	67688	74188	74088	67788
357039	EM	67689	74189	74089	67789
357040	EM	67690	74190	74090	67790
357041	EM	67691	74191	74091	67791
357042	EM	67692	74192	74092	67792
357043	EM	67693	74193	74093	67793
357044	EM	67694	74194	74094	67794
357045	EM	67695	74195	74095	67795
357046	EM	67696	74196	74096	67796

357001 BARRY FLAXMAN. 357002 ARTHUR LEWIS STRIDE 1841-1922. 357003 SOUTHEND city.on.sea. 357004 TONY AMOS. 357006 DIAMOND JUBILEE 1952-2012. 357011 JOHN LOWING. 357016 TONY SMITH. 357028 London,Tilbury and Southend Railway 1854-2004.
357029 THOMAS WHITELEGG 1840-1922. 357030 ROBERT HARBEN WHITELEGG 1871-1957.

Class 357/2 Adtranz/Bombardier Electrostar (Outer Suburban)

		DMSO	MSO	PTSO	DMSO
357201	EM	68601	74701	74601	68701
357202	EM	68602	74702	74602	68702
357203	EM	68603	74703	74603	68703
357204	EM	68604	74704	74604	68704
357205	EM	68605	74705	74605	68705
357206	EM	68606	74706	74606	68706
357207	EM	68607	74707	74607	68707
357208	EM	68608	74708	74608	68708
357209	EM	68609	74709	74609	68709
357210	EM	68610	74710	74610	68710
357211	EM	68611	74711	74611	68711
357212	EM	68612	74712	74612	68712
357213	EM	68613	74713	74613	68713
357214	EM	68614	74714	74614	68714
357215	EM	68615	74715	74615	68715
357216	EM	68616	74716	74616	68716
357217	EM	68617	74717	74617	68717
357218	EM	68618	74718	74618	68718
357219	EM	68619	74719	74619	68719
357220	EM	68620	74720	74620	68720

357221	EM	68621	74721	74621	68721	357225	EM	68625	74725	74625	68725
357222	EM	68622	74722	74622	68722	357226	EM	68626	74726	74626	68726
357223	EM	68623	74723	74623	68723	357227	EM	68627	74727	74627	68727
357224	EM	68624	74724	74624	68724	357228	EM	68628	74728	74628	68728

357201 KEN BIRD. 357202 KENNY MITCHELL. 357203 HENRY PUMFRETT. 357204 DEREK FOWERS. 357205 JOHN D'SILVA. 357206 MARTIN AUNGIER. 357207 JOHN PAGE. 357208 DAVE DAVIS. 357209 JAMES SNELLING. 357213 UPMINSTER I.E.C.C. 357217 ALLAN BURNELL.

Class 360/1 Siemens Desiro UK

		DMCO	PTSO	TSO	DMCO			DMCO	PTSO	TSO	DMCO
360101	IL	65551	72551	74551	68551	360112	IL	65562	72562	74562	68562
360102	IL	65552	72552	74552	68552	360113	IL	65563	72563	74563	68563
360103	IL	65553	72553	74553	68553	360114	IL	65564	72564	74564	68564
360104	IL	65554	72554	74554	68554	360115	IL	65565	72565	74565	68565
360105	IL	65555	72555	74555	68555	360116	IL	65566	72566	74566	68566
360106	IL	65556	72556	74556	68556	360117	IL	65567	72567	74567	68567
360107	IL	65557	72557	74557	68557	360118	IL	65568	72568	74568	68568
360108	IL	65558	72558	74558	68558	360119	IL	65569	72569	74569	68569
360109	IL	65559	72559	74559	68559	360120	IL	65570	72570	74570	68570
360110	IL	65560	72560	74560	68560	360121	IL	65571	72571	74571	68571
360111	IL	65561	72561	74561	68561						

Class 360/2 Siemens Desiro (semi-fast Heathrow Express)

		DMSO	PTSO	TSO	TSO	DMSO			DMSO	PTSO	TSO	TSO	DMSO
360201	OH	78431	63421	72431	72421	78441	360204	OH	78434	63424	72434	72424	78444
360202	OH	78432	63422	72432	72422	78442	360205	OH	78435	63425	72435	72425	78445
360203	OH	78433	63423	72433	72423	78443							

Class 365/5 ABB York Networker (Outer Suburban) (dual voltage)

		DMCO	TSO	PTSO	DMCO			DMCO	TSO	PTSO	DMCO
365501	HE	65894	72241	72240	65935	365508	HE	65901	72255	72254	65942
365502	HE	65895	72243	72242	65936	365509	HE	65902	72257	72256	65943
365503	HE	65896	72245	72244	65937	365510	HE	65903	72259	72258	65944
365504	HE	65897	72247	72246	65938	365511	HE	65904	72261	72260	65945
365505	HE	65898	72249	72248	65939	365512	HE	65905	72263	72262	65946
365506	HE	65899	72251	72250	65940	365513	HE	65906	72265	72264	65947
365507	HE	65900	72253	72252	65941	365514	HE	65907	72267	72266	65948

365515	HE	65908	72269	72268	65949	365529	HE	65922	72297	72296	65963
365516	HE	65909	72271	72270	65950	365530	HE	65923	72299	72298	65964
365517	HE	65910	72273	72272	65951	365531	HE	65924	72301	72300	65965
365518	HE	65911	72275	72274	65952	365532	HE	65925	72303	72302	65966
365519	HE	65912	72277	72276	65953	365533	HE	65926	72305	72304	65967
365520	HE	65913	72279	72278	65954	365534	HE	65927	72307	72306	65968
365521	HE	65914	72281	72280	65955	365535	HE	65928	72309	72308	65969
365522	HE	65915	72283	72282	65956	365536	HE	65929	72311	72310	65970
365523	HE	65916	72285	72284	65957	365537	HE	65930	72313	72312	65971
365524	HE	65917	72287	72286	65958	365538	HE	65931	72315	72314	65972
365525	HE	65918	72289	72288	65959	365539	HE	65932	72317	72316	65973
365527	HE	65920	72293	72292	65961	365540	HE	65933	72319	72318	65974
365528	HE	65921	72295	72294	65962	365541	HE	65934	72321	72320	65975

Spare vehicle 65919 at ZN

365506 The Royston Express. 365513 Hornsey Depot. 365514 Captain George Vancouver. 365518 The Fenman.
365527 Robert Stripe Passengers' Champion. 365530 The Intalink Partnership.
365536 Rufus Barnes, Chief Executive of London TravelWatch for 25 years.
365537 Daniel Edwards (1974-2010) Cambridge Driver.

Class 375/3 Adtranz/Bombardier Electrostar (Outer Suburban)

		DMCO	TSO	DMCO			DMCO	TSO	DMCO
375301	RM	67921	74351	67931	375306	RM	67926	74356	67936
375302	RM	67922	74352	67932	375307	RM	67927	74357	67937
375303	RM	67923	74353	67933	375308	RM	67928	74358	67938
375304	RM	67924	74354	67934	375309	RM	67929	74359	67939
375305	RM	67925	74355	67935	375310	RM	67930	74360	67940

375304 Medway Valley Line 1856 -2006.

Class 375/6 Adtranz/Bombardier Electrostar (Express) Dual Voltage

		DMCO	MSO	PTSO	DMCO			DMCO	MSO	PTSO	DMCO
375601	RM	67801	74251	74201	67851	375609	RM	67809	74259	74209	67859
375602	RM	67802	74252	74202	67852	375610	RM	67810	74260	74210	67860
375603	RM	67803	74253	74203	67853	375611	RM	67811	74261	74211	67861
375604	RM	67804	74254	74204	67854	375612	RM	67812	74262	74212	67862
375605	RM	67805	74255	74205	67855	375613	RM	67813	74263	74213	67863
375606	RM	67806	74256	74206	67856	375614	RM	67814	74264	74214	67864
375607	RM	67807	74257	74207	67857	375615	RM	67815	74265	74215	67865
375608	RM	67808	74258	74208	67858	375616	RM	67816	74266	74216	67866

375617	RM	67817	74267	74217	67867	375624	RM	67824	74274	74224	67874
375618	RM	67818	74268	74218	67868	375625	RM	67825	74275	74225	67875
375619	RM	67819	74269	74219	67869	375626	RM	67826	74276	74226	67876
375620	RM	67820	74270	74220	67870	375627	RM	67827	74277	74227	67877
375621	RM	67821	74271	74221	67871	375628	RM	67828	74278	74228	67878
375622	RM	67822	74272	74222	67872	375629	RM	67829	74279	74229	67879
375623	RM	67823	74273	74223	67873	375630	RM	67830	74280	74230	67880

375608 BROMLEY TRAVELWISE. 375610 Royal Tunbridge Wells. 375611 DR WILLIAM HARVEY. 375619 DRIVER JOHN NEVE. 375623 HOSPICE IN THE WEALD.

Class 375/7 Bombardier Electrostar Express Dual Voltage

		DMCO	MSO	TSO	DMCO			DMCO	MSO	TSO	DMCO
375701	RM	67831	74281	74231	67881	375709	RM	67839	74289	74239	67889
375702	RM	67832	74282	74232	67882	375710	RM	67840	74290	74240	67890
375703	RM	67833	74283	74233	67883	375711	RM	67841	74291	74241	67891
375704	RM	67834	74284	74234	67884	375712	RM	67842	74292	74242	67892
375705	RM	67835	74285	74235	67885	375713	RM	67843	74293	74243	67893
375706	RM	67836	74286	74236	67886	375714	RM	67844	74294	74244	67894
375707	RM	67837	74287	74237	67887	375715	RM	67845	74295	74245	67895
375708	RM	67838	74288	74238	67888						

375701 KENT AIR AMBULANCE EXPLORER.

Class 375/8 Bombardier Electrostar (EXPRESS) Dual Voltage

		DMCO	MSO	TSO	DMCO			DMCO	MSO	TSO	DMCO
375801	RM	73301	79001	78201	73701	375816	RM	73316	79016	78216	73716
375802	RM	73302	79002	78202	73702	375817	RM	73317	79017	78217	73717
375803	RM	73303	79003	78203	73703	375818	RM	73318	79018	78218	73718
375804	RM	73304	79004	78204	73704	375819	RM	73319	79019	78219	73719
375805	RM	73305	79005	78205	73705	375820	RM	73320	79020	78220	73720
375806	RM	73306	79006	78206	73706	375821	RM	73321	79021	78221	73721
375807	RM	73307	79007	78207	73707	375822	RM	73322	79022	78222	73722
375808	RM	73308	79008	78208	73708	375823	RM	73323	79023	78223	73723
375809	RM	73309	79009	78209	73709	375824	RM	73324	79024	78224	73724
375810	RM	73310	79010	78210	73710	375825	RM	73325	79025	78225	73725
375811	RM	73311	79011	78211	73711	375826	RM	73326	79026	78226	73726
375812	RM	73312	79012	78212	73712	375827	RM	73327	79027	78227	73727
375813	RM	73313	79013	78213	73713	375828	RM	73328	79028	78228	73728
375814	RM	73314	79014	78214	73714	375829	RM	73329	79029	78229	73729
375815	RM	73315	79015	78215	73715	375830	RM	73330	79030	78230	73730

375830 City of London.

Class 375/9 Bombardier Electrostar (Outer Suburban) Dual Voltage

		DMCO	MSO	TSO	DMCO			DMCO	MSO	TSO	DMCO
375901	RM	73331	79031	79061	73731	375915	RM	73345	79045	79075	73745
375902	RM	73332	79032	79062	73732	375916	RM	73346	79046	79076	73746
375903	RM	73333	79033	79063	73733	375917	RM	73347	79047	79077	73747
375904	RM	73334	79034	79064	73734	375918	RM	73348	79048	79078	73748
375905	RM	73335	79035	79065	73735	375919	RM	73349	79049	79079	73749
375906	RM	73336	79036	79066	73736	375920	RM	73350	79050	79080	73750
375907	RM	73337	79037	79067	73737	375921	RM	73351	79051	79081	73751
375908	RM	73338	79038	79068	73738	375922	RM	73352	79052	79082	73752
375909	RM	73339	79039	79069	73739	375923	RM	73353	79053	79083	73753
375910	RM	73340	79040	79070	73740	375924	RM	73354	79054	79084	73754
375911	RM	73341	79041	79071	73741	375925	RM	73355	79055	79085	73755
375912	RM	73342	79042	79072	73742	375926	RM	73356	79056	79086	73756
375913	RM	73343	79043	79073	73743	375927	RM	73357	79057	79087	73757
375914	RM	73344	79044	79074	73744						

Class 376 Bombardier Derby Electrostar (Inner Suburban)

		DMSO	MSO	TSO	MSO	DMSO			DMSO	MSO	TSO	MSO	DMSO
376001	SG	61101	63301	64301	63501	61601	376019	SG	61119	63319	64319	63519	61619
376002	SG	61102	63302	64302	63502	61602	376020	SG	61120	63320	64320	63520	61620
376003	SG	61103	63303	64303	63503	61603	376021	SG	61121	63321	64321	63521	61621
376004	SG	61104	63304	64304	63504	61604	376022	SG	61122	63322	64322	63522	61622
376005	SG	61105	63305	64305	63505	61605	376023	SG	61123	63323	64323	63523	61623
376006	SG	61106	63306	64306	63506	61606	376024	SG	61124	63324	64324	63524	61624
376007	SG	61107	63307	64307	63507	61607	376025	SG	61125	63325	64325	63525	61625
376008	SG	61108	63308	64308	63508	61608	376026	SG	61126	63326	64326	63526	61626
376009	SG	61109	63309	64309	63509	61609	376027	SG	61127	63327	64327	63527	61627
376010	SG	61110	63310	64310	63510	61610	376028	SG	61128	63328	64328	63528	61628
376011	SG	61111	63311	64311	63511	61611	376029	SG	61129	63329	64329	63529	61629
376012	SG	61112	63312	64312	63512	61612	376030	SG	61130	63330	64330	63530	61630
376013	SG	61113	63313	64313	63513	61613	376031	SG	61131	63331	64331	63531	61631
376014	SG	61114	63314	64314	63514	61614	376032	SG	61132	63332	64332	63532	61632
376015	SG	61115	63315	64315	63515	61615	376033	SG	61133	63333	64333	63533	61633
376016	SG	61116	63316	64316	63516	61616	376034	SG	61134	63334	64334	63534	61634
376017	SG	61117	63317	64317	63517	61617	376035	SG	61135	63335	64335	63535	61635
376018	SG	61118	63318	64318	63518	61618	376036	SG	61136	63336	64336	63536	61636

Class 377/1 Bombardier Electrostar (Express & Outer Suburban)

		DMCO	MSO	TSO	DMCO			DMCO	MSO	TSO	DMCO
377101	BI	78501	77101	78901	78701	377133	BI	78533	77133	78933	78733
377102	BI	78502	77102	78902	78702	377134	BI	78534	77134	78934	78734
377103	BI	78503	77103	78903	78703	377135	BI	78535	77135	78935	78735
377104	BI	78504	77104	78904	78704	377136	BI	78536	77136	78936	78736
377105	BI	78505	77105	78905	78705	377137	BI	78537	77137	78937	78737
377106	BI	78506	77106	78906	78706	377138	BI	78538	77138	78938	78738
377107	BI	78507	77107	78907	78707	377139	BI	78539	77139	78939	78739
377108	BI	78508	77108	78908	78708	377140	BI	78540	77140	78940	78740
377109	BI	78509	77109	78909	78709	377141	BI	78541	77141	78941	78741
377110	BI	78510	77110	78910	78710	377142	BI	78542	77142	78942	78742
377111	BI	78511	77111	78911	78711	377143	BI	78543	77143	78943	78743
377112	BI	78512	77112	78912	78712	377144	BI	78544	77144	78944	78744
377113	BI	78513	77113	78913	78713	377145	BI	78545	77145	78945	78745
377114	BI	78514	77114	78914	78714	377146	BI	78546	77146	78946	78746
377115	BI	78515	77115	78915	78715	377147	BI	78547	77147	78947	78747
377116	BI	78516	77116	78916	78716	377148	BI	78548	77148	78948	78748
377117	BI	78517	77117	78917	78717	377149	BI	78549	77149	78949	78749
377118	BI	78518	77118	78918	78718	377150	BI	78550	77150	78950	78750
377119	BI	78519	77119	78919	78719	377151	BI	78551	77151	78951	78751
377120	BI	78520	77120	78920	78720	377152	BI	78552	77152	78952	78752
377121	BI	78521	77121	78921	78721	377153	BI	78553	77153	78953	78753
377122	BI	78522	77122	78922	78722	377154	BI	78554	77154	78954	78754
377123	BI	78523	77123	78923	78723	377155	BI	78555	77155	78955	78755
377124	BI	78524	77124	78924	78724	377156	BI	78556	77156	78956	78756
377125	BI	78525	77125	78925	78725	377157	BI	78557	77157	78957	78757
377126	BI	78526	77126	78926	78726	377158	BI	78558	77158	78958	78758
377127	BI	78527	77127	78927	78727	377159	BI	78559	77159	78959	78759
377128	BI	78528	77128	78928	78728	377160	BI	78560	77160	78960	78760
377129	BI	78529	77129	78929	78729	377161	BI	78561	77161	78961	78761
377130	BI	78530	77130	78930	78730	377162	BI	78562	77162	78962	78762
377131	BI	78531	77131	78931	78731	377163	BI	78563	77163	78963	78763
377132	BI	78532	77132	78932	78732	377164	BI	78564	77164	78964	78764

Class 377/2 Bombardier Derby Electrostar dual voltage

		DMCO	MSO	PTSO	DMCO			DMCO	MSO	PTSO	DMCO
377201	SU	78571	77171	78971	78771	377207	BF	78577	77177	78977	78777
377202	SU	78572	77172	78972	78772	377208	SU	78578	77178	78978	78778
377203	SU	78573	77173	78973	78773	377209	SU	78579	77179	78979	78779
377204	SU	78574	77174	78974	78774	377210	SU	78580	77180	78980	78780
377205	SU	78575	77175	78975	78775	377211	BF	78581	77181	78981	78781
377206	SU	78576	77176	78976	78776	377212	BF	78582	77182	78982	78782

377213	SU	78583	77183	78983	78783	377215	SU	78585	77185	78985	78785
377214	SU	78584	77184	78984	78784						

Class 377/3 Bombardier Derby Electrostar

		DMCO	TSO	DMCO			DMCO	TSO	DMCO
377301	SU	68201	74801	68401	377315	SU	68215	74815	68415
377302	SU	68202	74802	68402	377316	SU	68216	74816	68416
377303	SU	68203	74803	68403	377317	SU	68217	74817	68417
377304	SU	68204	74804	68404	377318	SU	68218	74818	68418
377305	SU	68205	74805	68405	377319	SU	68219	74819	68419
377306	SU	68206	74806	68406	377320	SU	68220	74820	68420
377307	SU	68207	74807	68407	377321	SU	68221	74821	68421
377308	SU	68208	74808	68408	377322	SU	68222	74822	68422
377309	SU	68209	74809	68409	377323	SU	68223	74823	68423
377310	SU	68210	74810	68410	377324	SU	68224	74824	68424
377311	SU	68211	74811	68411	377325	SU	68225	74825	68425
377312	SU	68212	74812	68412	377326	SU	68226	74826	68426
377313	SU	68213	74813	68413	377327	SU	68227	74827	68427
377314	SU	68214	74814	68414	377328	SU	68228	74828	68428

Class 377/4 Bombardier Derby Electrostar (Outer Suburban)

		DMCO	MSO	TSO	DMCO			DMCO	MSO	TSO	DMCO
377401	BI	73401	78801	78601	73801	377420	BI	73420	78820	78620	73820
377402	BI	73402	78802	78602	73802	377421	BI	73421	78821	78621	73821
377403	BI	73403	78803	78603	73803	377422	BI	73422	78822	78622	73822
377404	BI	73404	78804	78604	73804	377423	BI	73423	78823	78623	73823
377405	BI	73405	78805	78605	73805	377424	BI	73424	78824	78624	73824
377406	BI	73406	78806	78606	73806	377425	BI	73425	78825	78625	73825
377407	BI	73407	78807	78607	73807	377426	BI	73426	78826	78626	73826
377408	BI	73408	78808	78608	73808	377427	BI	73427	78827	78627	73827
377409	BI	73409	78809	78609	73809	377428	BI	73428	78828	78628	73828
377410	BI	73410	78810	78610	73810	377429	BI	73429	78829	78629	73829
377411	BI	73411	78811	78611	73811	377430	BI	73430	78830	78630	73830
377412	BI	73412	78812	78612	73812	377431	BI	73431	78831	78631	73831
377413	BI	73413	78813	78613	73813	377432	BI	73432	78832	78632	73832
377414	BI	73414	78814	78614	73814	377433	BI	73433	78833	78633	73833
377415	BI	73415	78815	78615	73815	377434	BI	73434	78834	78634	73834
377416	BI	73416	78816	78616	73816	377435	BI	73435	78835	78635	73835
377417	BI	73417	78817	78617	73817	377436	BI	73436	78836	78636	73836
377418	BI	73418	78818	78618	73818	377437	BI	73437	78837	78637	73837
377419	BI	73419	78819	78619	73819	377438	BI	73438	78838	78638	73838

377439	BI	73439	78839	78639	73839
377440	BI	73440	78840	78640	73840
377441	BI	73441	78841	78641	73841
377442	BI	73442	78842	78642	73842
377443	BI	73443	78843	78643	73843
377444	BI	73444	78844	78644	73844
377445	BI	73445	78845	78645	73845
377446	BI	73446	78846	78646	73846
377447	BI	73447	78847	78647	73847
377448	BI	73448	78848	78648	73848
377449	BI	73449	78849	78649	73849
377450	BI	73450	78850	78650	73850
377451	BI	73451	78851	78651	73851
377452	BI	73452	78852	78652	73852
377453	BI	73453	78853	78653	73853
377454	BI	73454	78854	78654	73854
377455	BI	73455	78855	78655	73855
377456	BI	73456	78856	78656	73856
377457	BI	73457	78857	78657	73857
377458	BI	73458	78858	78658	73858
377459	BI	73459	78859	78659	73859
377460	BI	73460	78860	78660	73860
377461	BI	73461	78861	78661	73861
377462	BI	73462	78862	78662	73862
377463	BI	73463	78863	78663	73863
377464	BI	73464	78864	78664	73864
377465	BI	73465	78865	78665	73865
377466	BI	73466	78866	78666	73866
377467	BI	73467	78867	78667	73867
377468	BI	73468	78868	78668	73868
377469	BI	73469	78869	78669	73869
377470	BI	73470	78870	78670	73870
377471	BI	73471	78871	78671	73871
377472	BI	73472	78872	78672	73872
377473	BI	73473	78873	78673	73873
377474	BI	73474	78874	78674	73874
377475	BI	73475	78875	78675	73875

Class 377/5 Bombardier Electrostar

		DMCO	MSO	PTSO	DMCO
377501	BF	73501	75901	74901	73601
377502	BF	73502	75902	74902	73602
377503	BF	73503	75903	74903	73603
377504	BF	73504	75904	74904	73604
377505	BF	73505	75905	74905	73605
377506	BF	73506	75906	74906	73606
377507	BF	73507	75907	74907	73607
377508	BF	73508	75908	74908	73608
377509	BF	73509	75909	74909	73609
377510	BF	73510	75910	74910	73610
377511	BF	73511	75911	74911	73611
377512	BF	73512	75912	74912	73612
377513	BF	73513	75913	74913	73613
377514	BF	73514	75914	74914	73614
377515	BF	73515	75915	74915	73615
377516	BF	73516	75916	74916	73616
377517	BF	73517	75917	74917	73617
377518	BF	73518	75918	74918	73618
377519	BF	73519	75919	74919	73619
377520	BF	73520	75920	74920	73620
377521	BF	73521	75921	74921	73621
377522	BF	73522	75922	74922	73622
377523	BF	73523	75923	74923	73623

Class 377/6 (DC only) **Bombardier Electrostar (Suburban)** Southern due 2013

	DMSO	MSO	TSO	MSO	DMSO
377601	70101	70201	70301	70401	70501
377602	70102	70202	70302	70402	70502
377603	70103	70203	70303	70403	70503
377604	70104	70204	70304	70404	70504
377605	70105	70205	70305	70405	70505
377606	70106	70206	70306	70406	70506
377607	70107	70207	70307	70407	70507
377608	70108	70208	70308	70408	70508

377609	70109	70209	70309	70409	70509	377618	70118	70218	70318	70418	70518
377610	70110	70210	70310	70410	70510	377619	70119	70219	70319	70419	70519
377611	70111	70211	70311	70411	70511	377620	70120	70220	70320	70420	70520
377612	70112	70212	70312	70412	70512	377621	70121	70221	70321	70421	70521
377613	70113	70213	70313	70413	70513	377622	70122	70222	70322	70422	70522
377614	70114	70214	70314	70414	70514	377623	70123	70223	70323	70423	70523
377615	70115	70215	70315	70415	70515	377624	70124	70224	70324	70424	70524
377616	70116	70216	70316	70416	70516	377625	70125	70225	70325	70425	70525
377617	70117	70217	70317	70417	70517	377626	70126	70226	70326	70426	70526

Class 377/7 Bombardier Electrostar dual voltage on order for Southern

377701
377702
377703
377704
377705
377706
377707
377708

Class 378 Bombardier Derby Capitalstar (Suburban)

378/1 DC only

		DMSO	MSO	PTSO	DMSO			DMSO	MSO	PTSO	DMSO
378135	NG	38035	38235	38335	38135	378145	NG	38045	38245	38345	38145
378136	NG	38036	38236	38336	38136	378146	NG	38046	38246	38346	38146
378137	NG	38037	38237	38337	38137	378147	NG	38047	38247	38347	38147
378138	NG	38038	38238	38338	38138	378148	NG	38048	38248	38348	38148
378139	NG	38039	38239	38339	38139	378149	NG	38049	38249	38349	38149
378140	NG	38040	38240	38340	38140	378150	NG	38050	38250	38350	38150
378141	NG	38041	38241	38341	38141	378151	NG	38051	38251	38351	38151
378142	NG	38042	38242	38342	38142	378152	NG	38052	38252	38352	38152
378143	NG	38043	38243	38343	38143	378153	NG	38053	38253	38353	38153
378144	NG	38044	38244	38344	38144	378154	NG	38054	38254	38354	38154

Class 378/2 dual voltage

378201-224 were delivered as a 3 car and renumbered from 378001-024 when extra MSO was added

		DMSO	MSO	PTSO	DMSO			DMSO	MSO	PTSO	DMSO
378201	NG	38001	38201	38301	38101	378210	NG	38010	38210	38310	38110
378202	NG	38002	38202	38302	38102	378211	NG	38011	38211	38311	38111
378203	NG	38003	38203	38303	38103	378212	NG	38012	38212	38312	38112
378204	NG	38004	38204	38304	38104	378213	NG	38013	38213	38313	38113
378205	NG	38005	38205	38305	38105	378214	NG	38014	38214	38314	38114
378206	NG	38006	38206	38306	38106	378215	NG	38015	38215	38315	38115
378207	NG	38007	38207	38307	38107	378216	NG	38016	38216	38316	38116
378208	NG	38008	38208	38308	38108	378217	NG	38017	38217	38317	38117
378209	NG	38009	38209	38309	38109	378218	NG	38018	38218	38318	38118

378219	NG	38019	38219	38319	38119	378229	NG	38029	38229	38329	38129
378220	NG	38020	38220	38320	38120	378230	NG	38030	38230	38330	38130
378221	NG	38021	38221	38321	38121	378231	NG	38031	38231	38331	38131
378222	NG	38022	38222	38322	38122	378232	NG	38032	38232	38332	38132
378223	NG	38023	38223	38323	38123	378233	NG	38033	38233	38333	38133
378224	NG	38024	38224	38324	38124	378234	NG	38034	38234	38334	38134
378225	NG	38025	38225	38325	38125	378255	NG	38055	38255	38355	38155
378226	NG	38026	38226	38326	38126	378256	NG	38056	38256	38356	38156
378227	NG	38027	38227	38327	38127	378257	NG	38057	38257	38357	38157
378228	NG	38028	38228	38328	38128						

378233 Ian Brown CBE

Class 379 Bombardier Electrostar East Anglia

		DMSO	MSO	PTSO	DMCO			DMSO	MSO	PTSO	DMCO
379001	IL	61201	61701	61901	62101	379016	IL	61216	61716	61916	62116
379002	IL	61202	61702	61902	62102	379017	IL	61217	61717	61917	62117
379003	IL	61203	61703	61903	62103	379018	IL	61218	61718	61918	62118
379004	IL	61204	61704	61904	62104	379019	IL	61219	61719	61919	62119
379005	IL	61205	61705	61905	62105	379020	IL	61220	61720	61920	62120
379006	IL	61206	61706	61906	62106	379021	IL	61221	61721	61921	62121
379007	IL	61207	61707	61907	62107	379022	IL	61222	61722	61922	62122
379008	IL	61208	61708	61908	62108	379023	IL	61223	61723	61923	62123
379009	IL	61209	61709	61909	62109	379024	IL	61224	61724	61924	62124
379010	IL	61210	61710	61910	62110	379025	IL	61225	61725	61925	62125
379011	IL	61211	61711	61911	62111	379026	IL	61226	61726	61926	62126
379012	IL	61212	61712	61912	62112	379027	IL	61227	61727	61927	62127
379013	IL	61213	61713	61913	62113	379028	IL	61228	61728	61928	62128
379014	IL	61214	61714	61914	62114	379029	IL	61229	61729	61929	62129
379015	IL	61215	61715	61915	62115	379030	IL	61230	61730	61930	62130

379005 Stansted Express. 379011 Ely Cathedral. 379012 The West Anglian. 379015 City of Cambridge. 379025 Go Discover.

Class 380/0 Siemens Desiro UK ScotRail

		DMSO	PTSO	DMSO			DMSO	PTSO	DMSO
380001	GW	38501	38601	38701	380006	GW	38506	38606	38706
380002	GW	38502	38602	38702	380007	GW	38507	38607	38707
380003	GW	38503	38603	38703	380008	GW	38508	38608	38708
380004	GW	38504	38604	38704	380009	GW	38509	38609	38709
380005	GW	38505	38605	38705	380010	GW	38510	38610	38710

380011	GW	38511	38611	38711	380017	GW	38517	38617	38717
380012	GW	38512	38612	38712	380018	GW	38518	38618	38718
380013	GW	38513	38613	38713	380019	GW	38519	38619	38719
380014	GW	38514	38614	38714	380020	GW	38520	38620	38720
380015	GW	38515	38615	38715	380021	GW	38521	38621	38721
380016	GW	38516	38616	38716	380022	GW	38522	38622	38722

380/1

		DMSO	PTSO	TSO	DMSO			DMSO	PTSO	TSO	DMSO
380101	GW	38551	38651	38851	38751	380109	GW	38559	38659	38859	38759
380102	GW	38552	38652	38852	38752	380110	GW	38560	38660	38860	38760
380103	GW	38553	38653	38853	38753	380111	GW	38561	38661	38861	38761
380104	GW	38554	38654	38854	38754	380112	GW	38562	38662	38862	38762
380105	GW	38555	38655	38855	38755	380113	GW	38563	38663	38863	38763
380106	GW	38556	38656	38856	38756	380114	GW	38564	38664	38864	38764
380107	GW	38557	38657	38857	38757	380115	GW	38565	38665	38865	38765
380108	GW	38558	38658	38858	38758	380116	GW	38566	38666	38866	38766

Class 390 Alstom Pendolino-Britannico Tilting

		DMRFO	MFO	PTFO	MFO	TSO	MSO	TSO	MSO	PTSRMB	MSO	DMSO
390001	MA	69101	69401	69501	69601			68801	69701	69801	69901	69201
390002	MA	69102	69402	69502	69602			68802	69702	69802	69902	69202
390005	MA	69105	69405	69505	69605			68805	69705	69805	69905	69205
390006	MA	69106	69406	69506	69606			68806	69706	69806	69906	69206
390008	MA	69108	69408	69508	69608			68808	69708	69808	69908	69208
390009	MA	69109	69409	69509	69609			68809	69709	69809	69909	69209
390010	MA	69110	69410	69510	69610			68810	69710	69810	69910	69210
390011	MA	69111	69411	69511	69611			68811	69711	69811	69911	69211
390013	MA	69113	69413	69513	69613			68813	69713	69813	69913	69213
390016	MA	69116	69416	69516	69616			68816	69716	69816	69916	69216
390020	MA	69120	69420	69520	69620			68820	69720	69820	69920	69220
390039	MA	69139	69439	69539	69639			68839	69739	69839	69939	69239
390040	MA	69140	69440	69540	69640			68840	69740	69840	69940	69240
390042	MA	69142	69442	69542	69642			68842	69742	69842	69942	69242
390043	MA	69143	69443	69543	69643			68843	69743	69843	69943	69243
390044	MA	69144	69444	69544	69644			68844	69744	69844	69944	69244
390045	MA	69145	69445	69545	69645			68845	69745	69845	69945	69245
390046	MA	69146	69446	69546	69646			68846	69746	69846	69946	69246
390047	MA	69147	69447	69547	69647			68847	69747	69847	69947	69247
390049	MA	69149	69449	69549	69649			68849	69749	69849	69949	69249
390050	MA	69150	69450	69550	69650			68850	69750	69850	69950	69250
390103	MA	69103	69403	69503	69603	65303	68903	68803	69703	69803	69903	69203

390104	MA	69104	69404	69504	69604	65304	68904	68804	69704	69804	69904	69204
390107	MA	69107	69407	69507	69607	65307	68907	68807	69707	69807	69907	69207
390112	MA	69112	69412	69512	69612	65312	68912	68812	69712	69812	69912	69212
390114	MA	69114	69414	69514	69614	65314	68914	68814	69714	69814	69914	69214
390115	MA	69115	69415	69515	69615	65315	68915	68815	69715	69815	69915	69215
390117	MA	69117	69417	69517	69617	65317	68917	68817	69717	69817	69917	69217
390118	MA	69118	69418	69518	69618	65318	68918	68818	69718	69818	69918	69218
390119	MA	69119	69419	69519	69619	65319	68919	68819	69719	69819	69919	69219
390121	MA	69121	69421	69521	69621	65321	68921	68821	69721	69821	69921	69221
390122	MA	69122	69422	69522	69622	65322	68922	68822	69722	69822	69922	69222
390123	MA	69123	69423	69523	69623	65323	68923	68823	69723	69823	69923	69223
390124	MA	69124	69424	69524	69624	65324	68924	68824	69724	69824	69924	69224
390125	MA	69125	69425	69525	69625	65325	68925	68825	69725	69825	69925	69225
390126	MA	69126	69426	69526	69626	65326	68926	68826	69726	69826	69926	69226
390127	MA	69127	69427	69527	69627	65327	68927	68827	69727	69827	69927	69227
390128	MA	69128	69428	69528	69628	65328	68928	68828	69728	69828	69928	69228
390129	MA	69129	69429	69529	69629	65329	68929	68829	69729	69829	69929	69229
390130	MA	69130	69430	69530	69630	65330	68930	68830	69730	69830	69930	69230
390131	MA	69131	69431	69531	69631	65331	68931	68831	69731	69831	69931	69231
390132	MA	69132	69432	69532	69632	65332	68932	68832	69732	69832	69932	69232
390134	MA	69134	69434	69534	69634	65334	68934	68834	69734	69834	69934	69234
390135	MA	69135	69435	69535	69635	65335	68935	68835	69735	69835	69935	69235
390136	MA	69136	69436	69536	69636	65336	68936	68836	69736	69836	69936	69236
390137	MA	69137	69437	69537	69637	65337	68937	68837	69737	69837	69937	69237
390138	MA	69138	69438	69538	69638	65338	68938	68838	69738	69838	69938	69238
390141	MA	69141	69441	69541	69641	65341	68941	68841	69741	69841	69941	69241
390148	MA	69148	69448	69548	69648	65348	68948	68848	69748	69848	69948	69248
390151	MA	69151	69451	69551	69651	65351	68951	68851	69751	69851	69951	69251
390152	MA	69152	69452	69552	69652	65352	68952	68852	69752	69852	69952	69252
390153	MA	69153	69453	69553	69653	65353	68953	68853	69753	69853	69953	69253
390154	MA	69154	69454	69554	69654	65354	68954	68854	69754	69854	69954	69254
390155	MA	69155	69455	69555	69655	65355	68955	68855	69755	69855	69955	69255
390156	MA	69156	69456	69556	69656	65356	68956	68856	69756	69856	69956	69256
390157	MA	69157	69457	69557	69657	65357	68957	68857	69757	69857	69957	69257

Names: 01 Virgin Pioneer. 02 Virgin Angel. 03 Virgin Hero. 04 Alstom Pendolino. 05 City of Wolverhampton. 06 Tate Liverpool. 07 Virgin Lady. 08 Virgin King. 09 Treaty of Union. 10 A Decade of Progress. 11 City of Lichfield. 12 Virgin Star. 13 Virgin Spirit. 14 City of Manchester. 15 Virgin Crusader. 16 Virgin Champion. 17 Virgin Prince. 18 Virgin Princess. 19 Virgin Warrior. 20 Virgin Cavalier. 21 Virgin Dream. 22 Penny the Pendolino. 23 Virgin Glory. 24 Virgin Venturer. 25 Virgin Stagecoach. 26 Virgin Enterprise. 27 Virgin Buccaneer. 28 City of Preston. 29 City of Stoke on Trent. 30 City of Edinburgh. 31 City of Liverpool. 32 City of Birmingham. 34 City of Carlisle. 35 City of Lancaster. 36 City of Coventry. 37 Virgin Difference. 38 City of London. 39 Virgin Quest. 40 Virgin Pathfinder. 41 City of Chester. 42 City of Bangor/Dinas Bangor. 43 Virgin Explorer. 44 Virgin Lionheart. 45 101 Squadron. 46 Virgin Soldiers. 47 CLIC Sargent. 48 Virgin Harrier. 49 Virgin Express. 50 Virgin Invader. 51 Virgin Ambassador. 52 Virgin Knight. 53 Mission Accomplished. 57 Chad Varah.

Class 395 HITACHI HS1 (Dual Voltage)

		DTSO	MSO	MSO	MSO	MSO	DTSO	
395001	AD	39011	39012	39013	39014	39015	39016	Dame Kelly Holmes
395002	AD	39021	39022	39023	39024	39025	39026	Sebastian Coe
395003	AD	39031	39032	39033	39034	39035	39036	Sir Steve Redgrave
395004	AD	39041	39042	39043	39044	39045	39046	Sir Chris Hoy
395005	AD	39051	39052	39053	39054	39055	39056	Dame Tanni Grey-Thompson
395006	AD	39061	39062	39063	39064	39065	39066	Daley Thompson
395007	AD	39071	39072	39073	39074	39075	39076	Steve Backley
395008	AD	39081	39082	39083	39084	39085	39086	Ben Ainslie
395009	AD	39091	39092	39093	39094	39095	39096	Rebecca Adlington
395010	AD	39101	39102	39103	39104	39105	39106	
395011	AD	39111	39112	39113	39114	39115	39116	
395012	AD	39121	39122	39123	39124	39125	39126	
395013	AD	39131	39132	39133	39134	39135	39136	
395014	AD	39141	39142	39143	39144	39145	39146	
395015	AD	39151	39152	39153	39154	39155	39156	
395016	AD	39161	39162	39163	39164	39165	39166	Jamie Staff
395017	AD	39171	39172	39173	39174	39175	39176	Dame Sarah Storey
395018	AD	39181	39182	39183	39184	39185	39186	
395019	AD	39191	39192	39193	39194	39195	39196	
395020	AD	39201	39202	39203	39204	39205	39206	
395021	AD	39211	39212	39213	39214	39215	39216	
395022	AD	39221	39222	39223	39224	39225	39226	
395023	AD	39231	39232	39233	39234	39235	39236	
395024	AD	39241	39242	39243	39244	39245	39246	
395025	AD	39251	39252	39253	39254	39255	39256	
395026	AD	39261	39262	39263	39264	39265	39266	
395027	AD	39271	39272	39273	39274	39275	39276	Marc Woods
395028	AD	39281	39282	39283	39284	39285	39286	
395029	AD	39291	39292	39293	39294	39295	39296	

Class 442 BREL Derby

(some units do not carry the full number)

		DTF	TSO	MBLS	TSO	DTSO
442401	SL	77382	71818	62937	71842	77406
442402	SL	77383	71819	62938	71843	77407
442403	SL	77384	71820	62941	71844	77408
442404	SL	77385	71821	62939	71845	77409
442405	SL	77386	71822	62944	71846	77410
442406	SL	77389	71823	62942	71847	77411
442407	SL	77388	71824	62943	71848	77412
442408	SL	77387	71825	62945	71849	77413
442409	SL	77390	71826	62946	71850	77414
442410	SL	77391	71827	62948	71851	77415
442411	SL	77392	71828	62940	71858	77422
442412	SL	77393	71829	62947	71853	77417
442413	SL	77394	71830	62949	71854	77418
442414	SL	77395	71831	62950	71855	77419
442415	SL	77396	71832	62951	71856	77420
442416	SL	77397	71833	62952	71857	77421
442417	SL	77398	71834	62953	71852	77416
442418	SL	77399	71835	62954	71859	77423

442419	SL	77400	71836	62955	71860	77424	442422	SL	77403	71839	62958	71863	77427
442420	SL	77401	71837	62956	71861	77425	442423	SL	77404	71840	62959	71864	77428
442421	SL	77402	71838	62957	71862	77426	442424	SL	77405	71841	62960	71865	77429

Class 444 Siemens Desiro U.K. (Express)

		DMCO	TSO	TSO	PTSL	DMSO			DMCO	TSO	TSO	PTSL	DMSO
444001	NT	63801	67101	67151	67201	63851	444024	NT	63824	67124	67174	67224	63874
444002	NT	63802	67102	67152	67202	63852	444025	NT	63825	67125	67175	67225	63875
444003	NT	63803	67103	67153	67203	63853	444026	NT	63826	67126	67176	67226	63876
444004	NT	63804	67104	67154	67204	63854	444027	NT	63827	67127	67177	67227	63877
444005	NT	63805	67105	67155	67205	63855	444028	NT	63828	67128	67178	67228	63878
444006	NT	63806	67106	67156	67206	63856	444029	NT	63829	67129	67179	67229	63879
444007	NT	63807	67107	67157	67207	63857	444030	NT	63830	67130	67180	67230	63880
444008	NT	63808	67108	67158	67208	63858	444031	NT	63831	67131	67181	67231	63881
444009	NT	63809	67109	67159	67209	63859	444032	NT	63832	67132	67182	67232	63882
444010	NT	63810	67110	67160	67210	63860	444033	NT	63833	67133	67183	67233	63883
444011	NT	63811	67111	67161	67211	63861	444034	NT	63834	67134	67184	67234	63884
444012	NT	63812	67112	67162	67212	63862	444035	NT	63835	67135	67185	67235	63885
444013	NT	63813	67113	67163	67213	63863	444036	NT	63836	67136	67186	67236	63886
444014	NT	63814	67114	67164	67214	63864	444037	NT	63837	67137	67187	67237	63887
444015	NT	63815	67115	67165	67215	63865	444038	NT	63838	67138	67188	67238	63888
444016	NT	63816	67116	67166	67216	63866	444039	NT	63839	67139	67189	67239	63889
444017	NT	63817	67117	67167	67217	63867	444040	NT	63840	67140	67190	67240	63890
444018	NT	63818	67118	67168	67218	63868	444041	NT	63841	67141	67191	67241	63891
444019	NT	63819	67119	67169	67219	63869	444042	NT	63842	67142	67192	67242	63892
444020	NT	63820	67120	67170	67220	63870	444043	NT	63843	67143	67193	67243	63893
444021	NT	63821	67121	67171	67221	63871	444044	NT	63844	67144	67194	67244	63894
444022	NT	63822	67122	67172	67222	63872	444045	NT	63845	67145	67195	67245	63895
444023	NT	63823	67123	67173	67223	63873							

444001 NAOMI HOUSE. 444012 DESTINATION WEYMOUTH. 444018 THE FAB 444.

Class 450/0 & 450/5 HC Siemens Desiro U.K. (Outer Suburban)

		DMSO	TCO	TSO	DMSO			DMSO	TCO	TSO	DMSO
450001	NT	63201	64201	68101	63601	450008	NT	63208	64208	68108	63608
450002	NT	63202	64202	68102	63602	450009	NT	63209	64209	68109	63609
450003	NT	63203	64203	68103	63603	450010	NT	63210	64210	68110	63610
450004	NT	63204	64204	68104	63604	450011	NT	63211	64211	68111	63611
450005	NT	63205	64205	68105	63605	450012	NT	63212	64212	68112	63612
450006	NT	63206	64206	68106	63606	450013	NT	63213	64213	68113	63613
450007	NT	63207	64207	68107	63607	450014	NT	63214	64214	68114	63614

450015	NT	63215	64215	68115	63615	450090	NT	63290	64290	68190	63690
450016	NT	63216	64216	68116	63616	450091	NT	63291	64291	68191	63691
450017	NT	63217	64217	68117	63617	450092	NT	63292	64292	68192	63692
450018	NT	63218	64218	68118	63618	450093	NT	63293	64293	68193	63693
450019	NT	63219	64219	68119	63619	450094	NT	63294	64294	68194	63694
450020	NT	63220	64220	68120	63620	450095	NT	63295	64295	68195	63695
450021	NT	63221	64221	68121	63621	450096	NT	63296	64296	68196	63696
450022	NT	63222	64222	68122	63622	450097	NT	63297	64297	68197	63697
450023	NT	63223	64223	68123	63623	450098	NT	63298	64298	68198	63698
450024	NT	63224	64224	68124	63624	450099	NT	63299	64299	68199	63699
450025	NT	63225	64225	68125	63625	450100	NT	63300	64300	68200	63700
450026	NT	63226	64226	68126	63626	450101	NT	63751	66801	68851	63701
450027	NT	63227	64227	68127	63627	450102	NT	63752	66802	68852	63702
450028	NT	63228	64228	68128	63628	450103	NT	63753	66803	68853	63703
450029	NT	63229	64229	68129	63629	450104	NT	63754	66804	68854	63704
450030	NT	63230	64230	68130	63630	450105	NT	63755	66805	68855	63705
450031	NT	63231	64231	68131	63631	450106	NT	63756	66806	68856	63706
450032	NT	63232	64232	68132	63632	450107	NT	63757	66807	68857	63707
450033	NT	63233	64233	68133	63633	450108	NT	63758	66808	68858	63708
450034	NT	63234	64234	68134	63634	450109	NT	63759	66809	68859	63709
450035	NT	63235	64235	68135	63635	450110	NT	63760	66810	68860	63710
450036	NT	63236	64236	68136	63636	450111	NT	63901	63921	66901	66921
450037	NT	63237	64237	68137	63637	450112	NT	63902	63922	66902	66922
450038	NT	63238	64238	68138	63638	450113	NT	63903	63923	66903	66923
450039	NT	63239	64239	68139	63639	450114	NT	63904	63924	66904	66924
450040	NT	63240	64240	68140	63640	450115	NT	63905	63925	66905	66925
450041	NT	63241	64241	68141	63641	450116	NT	63906	63926	66906	66926
450042	NT	63242	64242	68142	63642	450117	NT	63907	63927	66907	66927
450071	NT	63271	64271	68171	63671	450118	NT	63908	63928	66908	66928
450072	NT	63272	64272	68172	63672	450119	NT	63909	63929	66909	66929
450073	NT	63273	64273	68173	63673	450120	NT	63910	63930	66910	66930
450074	NT	63274	64274	68174	63674	450121	NT	63911	63931	66911	66931
450075	NT	63275	64275	68175	63675	450122	NT	63912	63932	66912	66932
450076	NT	63276	64276	68176	63676	450123	NT	63913	63933	66913	66933
450077	NT	63277	64277	68177	63677	450124	NT	63914	63934	66914	66934
450078	NT	63278	64278	68178	63678	450125	NT	63915	63935	66915	66935
450079	NT	63279	64279	68179	63679	450126	NT	63916	63936	66916	66936
450080	NT	63280	64280	68180	63680	450127	NT	63917	63937	66917	66937
450081	NT	63281	64281	68181	63681	450543	NT	63243	64243	68143	63643
450082	NT	63282	64282	68182	63682	450544	NT	63244	64244	68144	63644
450083	NT	63283	64283	68183	63683	450545	NT	63245	64245	68145	63645
450084	NT	63284	64284	68184	63684	450546	NT	63246	64246	68146	63646
450085	NT	63285	64285	68185	63685	450547	NT	63247	64247	68147	63647
450086	NT	63286	64286	68186	63686	450548	NT	63248	64248	68148	63648
450087	NT	63287	64287	68187	63687	450549	NT	63249	64249	68149	63649
450088	NT	63288	64288	68188	63688	450550	NT	63250	64250	68150	63650
450089	NT	63289	64289	68189	63689	450551	NT	63251	64251	68151	63651

450552	NT	63252	64252	68152	63652	450562	NT	63262	64262	68162	63662
450553	NT	63253	64253	68153	63653	450563	NT	63263	64263	68163	63663
450554	NT	63254	64254	68154	63654	450564	NT	63264	64264	68164	63664
450555	NT	63255	64255	68155	63655	450565	NT	63265	64265	68165	63665
450556	NT	63256	64256	68156	63656	450566	NT	63266	64266	68166	63666
450557	NT	63257	64257	68157	63657	450567	NT	63267	64267	68167	63667
450558	NT	63258	64258	68158	63658	450568	NT	63268	64268	68168	63668
450559	NT	63259	64259	68159	63659	450569	NT	63269	64269	68169	63669
450560	NT	63260	64260	68160	63660	450570	NT	63270	64270	68170	63670
450561	NT	63261	64261	68161	63661						

Note: 450043-070 renumbered to 450543-570 and reclassified 450/5 High Capacity, TCO converted to TSO.
450015 DESIRO. 450042 TRELOAR COLLEGE. 450114 FAIRBRIDGE investing in the future.

Class 455/7 BR York (Inner Suburban) (carry numbers 5701-5750)

		DTSO	MSO	TSO	DTSO			DTSO	MSO	TSO	DTSO
455701	WD	77727	62783	71545	77728	455723	WD	77771	62805	71526	77772
455702	WD	77729	62784	71547	77730	455724	WD	77773	62806	71561	77774
455703	WD	77731	62785	71540	77732	455725	WD	77775	62807	71541	77776
455704	WD	77733	62786	71548	77734	455726	WD	77777	62808	71556	77778
455705	WD	77735	62787	71565	77736	455727	WD	77779	62809	71562	77780
455706	WD	77737	62788	71534	77738	455728	WD	77781	62810	71527	77782
455707	WD	77739	62789	71536	77740	455729	WD	77783	62811	71550	77784
455708	WD	77741	62790	71560	77742	455730	WD	77785	62812	71551	77786
455709	WD	77743	62791	71532	77744	455731	WD	77787	62813	71555	77788
455710	WD	77745	62792	71566	77746	455732	WD	77789	62814	71552	77790
455711	WD	77747	62793	71542	77748	455733	WD	77791	62815	71549	77792
455712	WD	77749	62794	71546	77750	455734	WD	77793	62816	71531	77794
455713	WD	77751	62795	71567	77752	455735	WD	77795	62817	71563	77796
455714	WD	77753	62796	71539	77754	455736	WD	77797	62818	71554	77798
455715	WD	77755	62797	71535	77756	455737	WD	77799	62819	71544	77800
455716	WD	77757	62798	71564	77758	455738	WD	77801	62820	71529	77802
455717	WD	77759	62799	71528	77760	455739	WD	77803	62821	71537	77804
455718	WD	77761	62800	71557	77762	455740	WD	77805	62822	71530	77806
455719	WD	77763	62801	71558	77764	455741	WD	77807	62823	71559	77808
455720	WD	77765	62802	71568	77766	455742	WD	77809	62824	71543	77810
455721	WD	77767	62803	71553	77768	455750	WD	77811	62825	71538	77812
455722	WD	77769	62804	71533	77770						

Class 455/8 BR York

		DTSO	MSO	TSO	DTSO
455801	SU	77627	62709	71657	77580
455802	SU	77581	62710	71664	77582
455803	SU	77583	62711	71639	77584
455804	SU	77585	62712	71640	77586
455805	SU	77587	62713	71641	77588
455806	SU	77589	62714	71642	77590
455807	SU	77591	62715	71643	77592
455808	SU	77637	62716	71644	77594
455809	SU	77623	62717	71648	77602
455810	SU	77597	62718	71646	77598
455811	SU	77599	62719	71647	77600
455812	SU	77595	62720	71645	77626
455813	SU	77603	62721	71649	77604
455814	SU	77605	62722	71650	77606
455815	SU	77607	62723	71651	77608
455816	SU	77609	62724	71652	77633
455817	SU	77611	62725	71653	77612
455818	SU	77613	62726	71654	77632
455819	SU	77615	62727	71637	77616
455820	SU	77617	62728	71656	77618
455821	SU	77619	62729	71655	77620
455822	SU	77621	62730	71658	77622
455823	SU	77601	62731	71659	77596
455824	SU	77593	62732	71660	77624
455825	SU	77579	62733	71661	77628
455826	SU	77630	62734	71662	77629
455827	SU	77610	62735	71663	77614
455828	SU	77631	62736	71638	77634
455829	SU	77635	62737	71665	77636
455830	SU	77625	62743	71666	77638
455831	SU	77639	62739	71667	77640
455832	SU	77641	62740	71668	77642
455833	SU	77643	62741	71669	77644
455834	SU	77645	62742	71670	77646
455835	SU	77647	62738	71671	77648
455836	SU	77649	62744	71672	77650
455837	SU	77651	62745	71673	77652

		DTSO	MSO	TSO	DTSO
455838	SU	77653	62746	71674	77654
455839	SU	77655	62747	71675	77656
455840	SU	77657	62748	71676	77658
455841	SU	77659	62749	71677	77660
455842	SU	77661	62750	71678	77662
455843	SU	77663	62751	71679	77664
455844	SU	77665	62752	71680	77666
455845	SU	77667	62753	71681	77668
455846	SU	77669	62754	71682	77670
455847	WD	77671	62755	71683	77672
455848	WD	77673	62756	71684	77674
455849	WD	77675	62757	71685	77676
455850	WD	77677	62758	71686	77678
455851	WD	77679	62759	71687	77680
455852	WD	77681	62760	71688	77682
455853	WD	77683	62761	71689	77684
455854	WD	77685	62762	71690	77686
455855	WD	77687	62763	71691	77688
455856	WD	77689	62764	71692	77690
455857	WD	77691	62765	71693	77692
455858	WD	77693	62766	71694	77694
455859	WD	77695	62767	71695	77696
455860	WD	77697	62768	71696	77698
455861	WD	77699	62769	71697	77700
455862	WD	77701	62770	71698	77702
455863	WD	77703	62771	71699	77704
455864	WD	77705	62772	71700	77706
455865	WD	77707	62773	71701	77708
455866	WD	77709	62774	71702	77710
455867	WD	77711	62775	71703	77712
455868	WD	77713	62776	71704	77714
455869	WD	77715	62777	71705	77716
455870	WD	77717	62778	71706	77718
455871	WD	77719	62779	71707	77720
455872	WD	77721	62780	71708	77722
455873	WD	77723	62781	71709	77724
455874	WD	77725	62782	71710	77726

Class 455/9 BR York/*Derby (carry numbers 5901-5920)

		DTSO	MSO	TSO	DTSO			DTSO	MSO	TSO	DTSO
455901	WD	77813	62826	71714	77814	455911	WD	77833	62836	71724	77834
455902	WD	77815	62827	71715	77816	455912	WD	77835	62837	67400*	77836
455903	WD	77817	62828	71716	77818	455913	ZN	77837	62838	71726	77838
455904	WD	77819	62829	71717	77820	455914	WD	77839	62839	71727	77840
455905	WD	77821	62830	71725	77822	455915	WD	77841	62840	71728	77842
455906	WD	77823	62831	71719	77824	455916	WD	77843	62841	71729	77844
455907	WD	77825	62832	71720	77826	455917	WD	77845	62842	71730	77846
455908	WD	77827	62833	71721	77828	455918	WD	77847	62843	71732	77848
455909	WD	77829	62834	71722	77830	455919	WD	77849	62844	71718	77850
455910	WD	77831	62835	71723	77832	455920	WD	77851	62845	71733	77852

Class 456 BREL York (Inner Suburban)

		DMSO	DTSO			DMSO	DTSO			DMSO	DTSO
456001	SU	64735	78250	456009	SU	64743	78258	456017	SU	64751	78266
456002	SU	64736	78251	456010	SU	64744	78259	456018	SU	64752	78267
456003	SU	64737	78252	456011	SU	64745	78260	456019	SU	64753	78268
456004	SU	64738	78253	456012	SU	64746	78261	456020	SU	64754	78269
456005	SU	64739	78254	456013	SU	64747	78262	456021	SU	64755	78270
456006	SU	64740	78255	456014	SU	64748	78263	456022	SU	64756	78271
456007	SU	64741	78256	456015	SU	64749	78264	456023	SU	64757	78272
456008	SU	64742	78257	456016	SU	64750	78265	456024	SU	64758	78273

456024 named Sir Cosmo Bonsor

Class 458 GEC - Alstom Juniper (Outer Suburban) (carry numbers 8001-8030)

		DMCO	TSO	MSO	DMCO			DMCO	TSO	MSO	DMCO
458001	WD	67601	74001	74101	67701	458013	WD	67613	74013	74113	67713
458002	WD	67602	74002	74102	67702	458014	WD	67614	74014	74114	67714
458003	WD	67603	74003	74103	67703	458015	WD	67615	74015	74115	67715
458004	WD	67604	74004	74104	67704	458016	WD	67616	74016	74116	67716
458005	WD	67605	74005	74105	67705	458017	WD	67617	74017	74117	67717
458006	WD	67606	74006	74106	67706	458018	WD	67618	74018	74118	67718
458007	WD	67607	74007	74107	67707	458019	WD	67619	74019	74119	67719
458008	WD	67608	74008	74108	67708	458020	WD	67620	74020	74121	67720
458009	WD	67609	74009	74109	67709	458021	WD	67621	74021	74122	67721
458010	WD	67610	74010	74110	67710	458022	WD	67622	74022	74123	67722
458011	WD	67611	74011	74111	67711	458023	WD	67623	74023	74124	67723
458012	WD	67612	74012	74112	67712	458024	WD	67624	74024	74124	67724

458025	WD 67625	74025	74125	67725	458028	WD 67628	74028	74128	67728
458026	WD 67626	74026	74126	67726	458029	WD 67629	74029	74129	67729
458027	WD 67627	74027	74127	67727	458030	WD 67630	74030	74130	67730

Class 458/5 Class 455/460 modified, refurbished by Alstom and Wabtec to make 36 units

4585xx

Class 460 (GEC)Alstom (Juniper) carry unit numbers 01-08 all now out of use

60 vehicles from 458 and 460 will be modified, refurbished by Alstom and Wabtec and inserted into 458 units creating a class of 36 five car units reclassified 458/5.

		DMLF	TFO	TCO	MSO	MSO	TSO	MSO	DMSO
460001	HQ	67901 LB	74401 LM	74411 LM	74421 LM	74431 LM	74441 LM	74451 LM	67911 LB
460002	HQ	67902 LB	74402 LM	74412 LM	74422 LM	74432 LM	74442 LM	74452 LM	67912 LB
460003	HQ	67903 LB	74403 LM	74413 LM	74423 LM	74433 LM	74443 LM	74453 LM	67913 LB
460004	HQ	67904 LB	74404 ZB	74414 ZB	74424 ZB	74434 ZB	74444 ZB	74454 ZB	67914 LB
460005	HQ	67905 LB	74405 LM	74415 LM	74425 LM	74435 LM	74445 LM	74455 LM	67915 LB
460006	HQ	67906 LB	74406 LM	74416 LM	74426 LM	74436 LM	74446 LM	74456 LM	67916 LB
460007	HQ	67907 LB	74407 LM	74417 LM	74427 LM	74437 LM	74447 LM	74457 LM	67917 LB
460008	HQ	67908 LB	74408 ZB	74418 ZB	74428 ZB	74438 ZB	74448 ZB	74458 ZB	67918 LB

Class 465/0 BREL/ABB York Networker (Suburban)

		DMSO	TSO	TSO	DMSO			DMSO	TSO	TSO	DMSO
465001	SG	64759	72028	72029	64809	465003	SG	64761	72032	72033	64811
465002	SG	64760	72030	72031	64810	465004	SG	64762	72034	72035	64812

465005	SG	64763	72036	72037	64813	465028	SG	64786	72082	72083	64836
465006	SG	64764	72038	72039	64814	465029	SG	64787	72084	72085	64837
465007	SG	64765	72040	72041	64815	465030	SG	64788	72086	72087	64838
465008	SG	64766	72042	72043	64816	465031	SG	64789	72088	72089	64839
465009	SG	64767	72044	72045	64817	465032	SG	64790	72090	72091	64840
465010	SG	64768	72046	72047	64818	465033	SG	64791	72092	72093	64841
465011	SG	64769	72048	72049	64819	465034	SG	64792	72094	72095	64842
465012	SG	64770	72050	72051	64820	465035	SG	64793	72096	72097	64843
465013	SG	64771	72052	72053	64821	465036	SG	64794	72098	72099	64844
465014	SG	64772	72054	72055	64822	465037	SG	64795	72100	72101	64845
465015	SG	64773	72056	72057	64823	465038	SG	64796	72102	72103	64846
465016	SG	64774	72058	72059	64824	465039	SG	64797	72104	72105	64847
465017	SG	64775	72060	72061	64825	465040	SG	64798	72106	72107	64848
465018	SG	64776	72062	72063	64826	465041	SG	64799	72108	72109	64849
465019	SG	64777	72064	72065	64827	465042	SG	64800	72110	72111	64850
465020	SG	64778	72066	72067	64828	465043	SG	64801	72112	72113	64851
465021	SG	64779	72068	72069	64829	465044	SG	64802	72114	72115	64852
465022	SG	64780	72070	72071	64830	465045	SG	64803	72116	72117	64853
465023	SG	64781	72072	72073	64831	465046	SG	64804	72118	72119	64854
465024	SG	64782	72074	72075	64832	465047	SG	64805	72120	72121	64855
465025	SG	64783	72076	72077	64833	465048	SG	64806	72122	72123	64856
465026	SG	64784	72078	72079	64834	465049	SG	64807	72124	72125	64857
465027	SG	64785	72080	72081	64835	465050	SG	64808	72126	72127	64858

465/1 BREL/ABB York Networker (Suburban)

		DMSO	TSO	TSO	DMSO			DMSO	TSO	TSO	DMSO
465151	SG	65800	72900	72901	65847	465169	SG	65818	72936	72937	65865
465152	SG	65801	72902	72903	65848	465170	SG	65819	72938	72939	65866
465153	SG	65802	72904	72905	65849	465171	SG	65820	72940	72941	65867
465154	SG	65803	72906	72907	65850	465172	SG	65821	72942	72943	65868
465155	SG	65804	72908	72909	65851	465173	SG	65822	72944	72945	65869
465156	SG	65805	72910	72911	65852	465174	SG	65823	72946	72947	65870
465157	SG	65806	72912	72913	65853	465175	SG	65824	72948	72949	65871
465158	SG	65807	72914	72915	65854	465176	SG	65825	72950	72951	65872
465159	SG	65808	72916	72917	65855	465177	SG	65826	72952	72953	65873
465160	SG	65809	72918	72919	65856	465178	SG	65827	72954	72955	65874
465161	SG	65810	72920	72921	65857	465179	SG	65828	72956	72957	65875
465162	SG	65811	72922	72923	65858	465180	SG	65829	72958	72959	65876
465163	SG	65812	72924	72925	65859	465181	SG	65830	72960	72961	65877
465164	SG	65813	72926	72927	65860	465182	SG	65831	72962	72963	65878
465165	SG	65814	72928	72929	65861	465183	SG	65832	72964	72965	65879
465166	SG	65815	72930	72931	65862	465184	SG	65833	72966	72967	65880
465167	SG	65816	72932	72933	65863	465185	SG	65834	72968	72969	65881
465168	SG	65817	72934	72935	65864	465186	SG	65835	72970	72971	65882

465187	SG	65836	72972	72973	65883	465193	SG	65842	72984	72985	65889
465188	SG	65837	72974	72975	65884	465194	SG	65843	72986	72987	65890
465189	SG	65838	72976	72977	65885	465195	SG	65844	72988	72989	65891
465190	SG	65839	72978	72979	65886	465196	SG	65845	72990	72991	65892
465191	SG	65840	72980	72981	65887	465197	SG	65846	72992	72993	65893
465192	SG	65841	72982	72983	65888						

Class 465/2 Metro Cammell Networker (Suburban)

		DMSO	TSO	TSO	DMSO			DMSO	TSO	TSO	DMSO
465235	SG	65734	72787	72788	65784	465243	SG	65742	72803	72804	65792
465236	SG	65735	72789	72790	65785	465244	SG	65743	72805	72806	65793
465237	SG	65736	72791	72792	65786	465245	SG	65744	72807	72808	65794
465238	SG	65737	72793	72794	65787	465246	SG	65745	72809	72810	65795
465239	SG	65738	72795	72796	65788	465247	SG	65746	72811	72812	65796
465240	SG	65739	72797	72798	65789	465248	SG	65747	72813	72814	65797
465241	SG	65740	72799	72800	65790	465249	SG	65748	72815	72816	65798
465242	SG	65741	72801	72802	65791	465250	SG	65749	72817	72818	65799

Class 465/9 Metro Cammell Networker (Suburban)

(Refurbished at Wabtec, Doncaster & renumbered from 465/2)

		DMCO	TSO	TSO	DMCO			DMCO	TSO	TSO	DMCO
465901	SG	65700	72719	72720	65750	465918	SG	65717	72753	72754	65767
465902	SG	65701	72721	72722	65751	465919	SG	65718	72755	72756	65768
465903	SG	65702	72723	72724	65752	465920	SG	65719	72757	72758	65769
465904	SG	65703	72725	72726	65753	465921	SG	65720	72759	72760	65770
465905	SG	65704	72727	72728	65754	465922	SG	65721	72761	72762	65771
465906	SG	65705	72729	72730	65755	465923	SG	65722	72763	72764	65772
465907	SG	65706	72731	72732	65756	465924	SG	65723	72765	72766	65773
465908	SG	65707	72733	72734	65757	465925	SG	65724	72767	72768	65774
465909	SG	65708	72735	72736	65758	465926	SG	65725	72769	72770	65775
465910	SG	65709	72737	72738	65759	465927	SG	65726	72771	72772	65776
465911	SG	65710	72739	72740	65760	465928	SG	65727	72773	72774	65777
465912	SG	65711	72741	72742	65761	465929	SG	65728	72775	72776	65778
465913	SG	65712	72743	72744	65762	465930	SG	65729	72777	72778	65779
465914	SG	65713	72745	72746	65763	465931	SG	65730	72779	72780	65780
465915	SG	65714	72747	72748	65764	465932	SG	65731	72781	72782	65781
465916	SG	65715	72749	72750	65765	465933	SG	65732	72783	72784	65782
465917	SG	65716	72751	72752	65766	465934	SG	65733	72785	72786	65783

465903 Remembrance.

Class 466/0 GEC-Alstom Networker (Suburban)

		DMSO	DTSO			DMSO	DTSO			DMSO	DTSO
466001	SG	64860	78312	466016	SG	64875	78327	466030	SG	64889	78341
466002	SG	64861	78313	466017	SG	64876	78328	466031	SG	64890	78342
466003	SG	64862	78314	466018	SG	64877	78329	466032	SG	64891	78343
466004	SG	64863	78315	466019	SG	64878	78330	466033	SG	64892	78344
466005	SG	64864	78316	466020	SG	64879	78331	466034	SG	64893	78345
466006	SG	64865	78317	466021	SG	64880	78332	466035	SG	64894	78346
466007	SG	64866	78318	466022	SG	64881	78333	466036	SG	64895	78347
466008	SG	64867	78319	466023	SG	64882	78334	466037	SG	64896	78348
466009	SG	64868	78320	466024	SG	64883	78335	466038	SG	64897	78349
466010	SG	64869	78321	466025	SG	64884	78336	466039	SG	64898	78350
466011	SG	64870	78322	466026	SG	64885	78337	466040	SG	64899	78351
466012	SG	64871	78323	466027	SG	64886	78338	466041	SG	64900	78352
466013	SG	64872	78324	466028	SG	64887	78339	466042	SG	64901	78353
466014	SG	64873	78325	466029	SG	64888	78340	466043	SG	64902	78354
466015	SG	64874	78326								

Class 483/0 Metro Cammell (Converted from London Underground stock)

		DMSO	DMSO			DMSO	DMSO			DMSO	DMSO
483002	RY	122	225	483006	RY	126	226	483008	RY	128	228
483004	RY	124	224	483007	RY	127	227	483009	RY	129	229

002 RAPTOR

488/3

		TSOH	TSO	TSOH	
8308	HQ	72614	72707	72615	i/user at DY.

Class 507 BREL York (Suburban)

		BDMSO	TSO	DMSO			BDMSO	TSO	DMSO
507001	BD	64367	71342	64405	507011	BD	64377	71352	64415
507002	BD	64368	71343	64406	507012	BD	64378	71353	64416
507003	BD	64369	71344	64407	507013	BD	64379	71354	64417
507004	BD	64388	71345	64408	507014	BD	64380	71355	64418
507005	BD	64371	71346	64409	507015	BD	64381	71356	64419
507006	BD	64372	71347	64410	507016	BD	64382	71357	64420
507007	BD	64373	71348	64411	507017	BD	64383	71358	64421
507008	BD	64374	71349	64412	507018	BD	64384	71359	64422
507009	BD	64375	71350	64413	507019	BD	64385	71360	64423
507010	BD	64376	71351	64414	507020	BD	64386	71361	64424

Unit	Depot			
507021	BD	64387	71362	64425
507023	BD	64389	71364	64427
507024	BD	64390	71365	64428
507025	BD	64391	71366	64429
507026	BD	64392	71367	64430
507027	BD	64393	71368	64431
507028	BD	64394	71369	64432
507029	BD	64395	71370	64433
507030	BD	64396	71371	64434
507031	BD	64397	71372	64435
507032	BD	64398	71373	64436
507033	BD	64399	71374	64437

507004 Bob Paisley. 507009 Dixie Dean. 507020 John Peel. 507021 Red Rum.
507023 Operations Inspector Stuart Mason. 507033 Councillor Jack Spriggs.

Class 508 BREL York (Suburban)

508/1

		DMSO	TSO	BDMSO
508103	BD	64651	71485	64694
508104	BD	64652	71486	64695
508108	BD	64656	71490	64699
508110	BD	64658	71492	64701
508111	BD	64659	71493	64702
508112	BD	64660	71494	64703
508114	BD	64662	71496	64705
508115	BD	64663	71497	64706
508117	BD	64665	71499	64708
508120	BD	64668	71502	64711
508122	BD	64670	71504	64713
508123	BD	64671	71505	64714
508124	BD	64672	71506	64715
508125	BD	64673	71507	64716
508126	BD	64674	71508	64717
508127	BD	64675	71509	64718
508128	BD	64676	71510	64719
508130	BD	64678	71512	64721
508131	BD	64679	71513	64722
508134	BD	64682	71516	64725
508136	BD	64684	71518	64727
508137	BD	64685	71519	64728
508138	BD	64686	71520	64729
508139	BD	64687	71521	64730
508140	BD	64688	71522	64731
508141	BD	64689	71523	64732
508143	BD	64691	71525	64734

508/2 (Facelifted/Refurbished at Wessex Traincare/Alstom, Eastleigh)

		DMSO	TSO	BDMSO
508201 (508101)	ZG	64649	71483	64692
508202 (508105)	ZG	64653	71487	64696
508203 (508106)	ZG	64654	71488	64697
508204 (508107)	ZG	64655	71489	64698
508205 (508109)	ZG	64657	71491	64700
508206 (508113)	ZG	64661	71495	64704
508207 (508116)	ZG	64664	71498	64707
508208 (508119)	ZG	64667	71501	64710
508209 (508121)	ZG	64669	71503	64712
508210 (508129)	ZG	64677	71515	64720
508211 (508132)	ZG	64680	71514	64723

508/3 (Facelifted/Refurbished at Wessex Traincare/Alstom, Eastleigh)

		DMSO	TSO	BDMSO
508301 (508102)	ZG	64650	71484	64693
508302 (508135)	ZG	64683	71517	64726
508303 (508142)	ZG	64690	71524	64733

Class 373 Eurostar Trains

British Sets

	DM	MS	TS	TS	TS	TS	RB	TF	TF	TBF
3001 TI	3730010	3730011	3730012	3730013	3730014	3730015	3730016	3730017	3730018	3730019
3002 TI	3730020	3730021	3730022	3730023	3730024	3730025	3730026	3730027	3730028	3730029
3003 TI	3730030	3730031	3730032	3730033	3730034	3730035	3730036	3730037	3730038	3730039
3004 TI	3730040	3730041	3730042	3730043	3730044	3730045	3730046	3730047	3730048	3730049
3005 TI	3730050	3730051	3730052	3730053	3730054	3730055	3730056	3730057	3730058	3730059
3006 TI	3730060	3730061	3730062	3730063	3730064	3730065	3730066	3730067	3730068	3730069
3007 TI	3730070	3730071	3730072	3730073	3730074	3730075	3730076	3730077	3730078	3730079
3008 TI	3730080	3730081	3730082	3730083	3730084	3730085	3730086	3730087	3730088	3730089
3009 TI	3730090	3730091	3730092	3730093	3730094	3730095	3730096	3730097	3730098	3730099
3010 TI	3730100	3730101	3730102	3730103	3730104	3730105	3730106	3730107	3730108	3730109
3011 TI	3730110	3730111	3730112	3730113	3730114	3730115	3730116	3730117	3730118	3730119
3012 TI	3730120	3730121	3730122	3730123	3730124	3730125	3730126	3730127	3730128	3730129
3013 TI	3730130	3730131	3730132	3730133	3730134	3730135	3730136	3730137	3730138	3730139
3014 TI	3730140	3730141	3730142	3730143	3730144	3730145	3730146	3730147	3730148	3730149
3015 TI	3730150	3730151	3730152	3730153	3730154	3730155	3730156	3730157	3730158	3730159
3016 TI	3730160	3730161	3730162	3730163	3730164	3730165	3730166	3730167	3730168	3730169
3017 TI	3730170	3730171	3730172	3730173	3730174	3730175	3730176	3730177	3730178	3730179
3018 TI	3730180	3730181	3730182	3730183	3730184	3730185	3730186	3730187	3730188	3730189
3019 TI	3730190	3730191	3730192	3730193	3730194	3730195	3730196	3730197	3730198	3730199
3020 TI	3730200	3730201	3730202	3730203	3730204	3730205	3730206	3730207	3730208	3730209
3021 TI	3730210	3730211	3730212	3730213	3730214	3730215	3730216	3730217	3730218	3730219
3022 TI	3730220	3730221	3730222	3730223	3730224	3730225	3730226	3730227	3730228	3730229

3001 Tread Lightly. 3002 Voyage Vert. 3003/04 Tri-City-Athlon 2010. 3007/08 Waterloo Sunset. 3009/10 REMEMBERING FROMELLES. 3013/14 LONDON 2012.

SNCB/NMBS Sets

	DM	MS	TS	TS	TS	TS	RB	TF	TF	TBF
3101 TI	3731010	3731011	3731012	3731013	3731004	3731015	3731016	3731017	3731018	3731019
3102 TI	3731020	3731021	3731022	3731023	3731024	3731025	3731026	3731027	3731028	3731029
3103 FF	3731030	3731031	3731032	3731033	3731034	3731035	3731036	3731037	3731038	3731039
3104 FF	3731040	3731041	3731042	3731043	3731044	3731045	3731046	3731047	3731048	3731049
3105 FF	3731050	3731051	3731052	3731053	3731054	3731055	3731056	3731057	3731058	3731059
3106 FF	3731060	3731061	3731062	3731063	3731064	3731065	3731066	3731067	3731068	3731069
3107 FF	3731070	3731071	3731072	3731073	3731074	3731075	3731076	3731077	3731078	3731079
3108 FF	3731080	3731081	3731082	3731083	3731084	3731085	3731086	3731087	3731088	3731089

SNCF Sets *French lines only

	DM	MS	TS	TS	TS	TS	RB	TF	TF	TBF
3201 LY	3732010	3732011	3732012	3732013	3732014	3732015	3732016	3732017	3732018	3732019
3202 LY	3732020	3732021	3732022	3732023	3732024	3732025	3732026	3732027	3732028	3732029
3203 LY*	3732030	3732031	3732032	3732033	3732034	3732035	3732036	3732037	3732038	3732039
3204 LY*	3732040	3732041	3732042	3732043	3732044	3732045	3732046	3732047	3732048	3732049
3205 LY	3732050	3732051	3732052	3732053	3732054	3732055	3732056	3732057	3732058	3732059
3206 LY	3732060	3732061	3732062	3732063	3732064	3732065	3732066	3732067	3732068	3732069
3207 LY	3732070	3732071	3732072	3732073	3732074	3732075	3732076	3732077	3732078	3732079
3208 LY	3732080	3732081	3732082	3732083	3732084	3732085	3732086	3732087	3732088	3732089
3209 LY	3732090	3732091	3732092	3732093	3732094	3732095	3732096	3732097	3732098	3732099
3210 LY	3732100	3732101	3732102	3732103	3732104	3732105	3732106	3732107	3732108	3732109
3211 LY	3732110	3732111	3732112	3732113	3732114	3732115	3732116	3732117	3732118	3732119
3212 LY	3732120	3732121	3732122	3732123	3732124	3732125	3732126	3732127	3732128	3732129
3213 LY	3732130	3732131	3732132	3732133	3732134	3732135	3732136	3732137	3732138	3732139
3214 LY	3732140	3732141	3732142	3732143	3732144	3732145	3732146	3732147	3732148	3732149
3215 LY	3732150	3732151	3732152	3732153	3732154	3732155	3732156	3732157	3732158	3732159
3216 LY	3732160	3732161	3732162	3732163	3732164	3732165	3732166	3732167	3732168	3732169
3217 LY	3732170	3732171	3732172	3732173	3732174	3732175	3732176	3732177	3732178	3732179
3218 LY	3732180	3732181	3732182	3732183	3732184	3732185	3732186	3732187	3732188	3732189
3219 LY	3732190	3732191	3732192	3732193	3732194	3732195	3732196	3732197	3732198	3732199
3220 LY	3732200	3732201	3732202	3732203	3732204	3732205	3732206	3732207	3732208	3732209
3221 LY	3732210	3732211	3732212	3732213	3732214	3732215	3732216	3732217	3732218	3732219
3222 LY	3732220	3732221	3732222	3732223	3732224	3732225	3732226	3732227	3732228	3732229
3223 LY	3732230	3732231	3732232	3732233	3732234	3732235	3732236	3732237	3732238	3732239
3224 LY	3732240	3732241	3732242	3732243	3732244	3732245	3732246	3732247	3732248	3732249
3225 LY*	3732250	3732251	3732252	3732253	3732254	3732255	3732256	3732257	3732258	3732259
3226 LY*	3732260	3732261	3732262	3732263	3732264	3732265	3732266	3732267	3732268	3732269
3227 LY*	3732270	3732271	3732272	3732273	3732274	3732275	3732276	3732277	3732278	3732279
3228 LY*	3732280	3732281	3732282	3732283	3732284	3732285	3732286	3732287	3732288	3732289
3229 LY	3732290	3732291	3732292	3732293	3732294	3732295	3732296	3732297	3732298	3732299
3230 LY	3732300	3732301	3732302	3732303	3732304	3732305	3732306	3732307	3732308	3732309
3231 LY	3732310	3732311	3732312	3732313	3732314	3732315	3732316	3732317	3732318	3732319
3232 LY	3732320	3732321	3732322	3732323	3732324	3732325	3732326	3732327	3732328	3732329

3207/08 MICHEL HOLLARD. 3209/10 THE DA VINCI CODE.

	DM	MS	TS	TS	TS	RB	TF	TBF
3301 LY	3733010	3733011	3733013	3733012	3733015	3733016	3733017	3733019
3302 LY	3733020	3733021	3733023	3733022	3733025	3733026	3733027	3733029
3303 LY	3733030	3733031	3733033	3733032	3733035	3733036	3733037	3733039
3304 LY	3733040	3733041	3733043	3733042	3733045	3733046	3733047	3733049
3305 LY	3733050	3733051	3733053	3733052	3733055	3733056	3733057	3733059
3306 LY	3733060	3733061	3733063	3733062	3733065	3733066	3733067	3733069
3307 LY	3733070	3733071	3733073	3733072	3733075	3733076	3733077	3733079

3308 TI	3733080	3733081	3733083	3733082	3733085	3733086	3733087	3733089
3309 LY	3733090	3733091	3733093	3733092	3733095	3733096	3733097	3733099
3310 LY	3733100	3733101	3733103	3733102	3733105	3733106	3733107	3733109
3311 LY	3733110	3733111	3733113	3733112	3733115	3733116	3733117	3733119
3312 LY	3733120	3733121	3733123	3733122	3733125	3733126	3733127	3733129
3313 LY	3733130	3733131	3733133	3733132	3733135	3733136	3733137	3733139
3314 LY	3733140	3733141	3733143	3733142	3733145	3733146	3733147	3733149

3313/14 named ENTENTE CORDIALE.

3303,3304 and four cars from 3307 and 3308 are stored.

3999 TI (Spare Motor Vehicle)

10 x e320 Eurostars on order, to be built in Germany

SERVICE UNITS

Current No.		Former No.	Description.	Allocation.
	3905		(76398,62266,70904,76397) Tractor Unit	AF
	3918		(76528,62321,70950,76527) Tractor Unit	AF
ADB	975600	10988}	930010 Mess Coach/Store (internal user)	DY
ADB	975601	10843}	930010 Training Coach (internal user)	DY
	977858	55024	Sandite/Route Learner 960010	TM
	977859	55025	Video Survey Unit 960011, PANDORA	AL (TS)
	977873	55022	Sandite Unit 960014 (L122)	AL
	977939	60145}	Sandite/Route Learner Unit 930301	SEu
	977940	60149}	930301	SEu
	977987	51371}		AL
	977988	51413}	Water Cannon Unit 960301	AL
	977992	51375}		AL
	999600	}	Class 150 CE Track Recording Train 950001	ZA
	999601	}	950001	ZA

DR	98901	98951	Multi Purpose Vehicle
DR	98902	98952	Multi Purpose Vehicle
DR	98903	98953	Multi Purpose Vehicle
DR	98904	98954	Multi Purpose Vehicle
DR	98905	98955	Multi Purpose Vehicle
DR	98906	98956	Multi Purpose Vehicle
DR	98907	98957	Multi Purpose Vehicle
DR	98908	98958	Multi Purpose Vehicle
DR	98909	98959	Multi Purpose Vehicle
DR	98910	98960	Multi Purpose Vehicle
DR	98911	98961	Multi Purpose Vehicle
DR	98912	98962	Multi Purpose Vehicle
DR	98913	98963	Multi Purpose Vehicle
DR	98914	98964	Multi Purpose Vehicle
DR	98915	98965	Multi Purpose Vehicle
DR	98916	98966	Multi Purpose Vehicle
DR	98917	98967	Multi Purpose Vehicle
DR	98918	98968	Multi Purpose Vehicle
DR	98919	98969	Multi Purpose Vehicle
DR	98920	98970	Multi Purpose Vehicle
DR	98921	98971	Multi Purpose Vehicle
DR	98922	98972	Multi Purpose Vehicle
DR	98923	98973	Multi Purpose Vehicle
DR	98924	98974	Multi Purpose Vehicle
DR	98925	98975	Multi Purpose Vehicle
DR	98926	98976	Multi Purpose Vehicle
DR	98927	98977	Multi Purpose Vehicle
DR	98928	98978	Multi Purpose Vehicle
DR	98929	98979	Multi Purpose Vehicle
DR	98930	98980	Multi Purpose Vehicle
DR	98931	98981	Multi Purpose Vehicle
DR	98932	98982	Multi Purpose Vehicle

COACHING STOCK

SAL (Caledonian Railway First Saloon)

41(99052/45018)CS

London & North Western Railway Dining Car **AO10**

159(99880)CS

Pullman Brake Third

232(99970) CAR NO. 79 NY

RFO (Restaurant First Open Mark 1) **AO40*/AJ11**

310* PEGASUS EH 324(99973) JOS de CRAU NY 325 DUART CP

Pullman Kitchen First/*Parlour First

318 ROBIN NY 326* EMERALD CS 328* OPAL NY

CK (Caledonian Railway Composite Corridor) **AO30**

464 BT

GNR Family Saloon **AO10**

807(99881)CS

RFO (Restaurant Buffet Open First Mark 2f) AJ1F

1200 AMBER	EH	1210	IS	1221	CS	1253	SH
1201	CS	1211	CS	1250	EH	1254	BH
1203	EH	1212	EH	1252	CS	1258	CS
1207	CS	1220	IS				

RKB (Restaurant Kitchen Buffet Mark 1) AK51

1566 CP (Car No. 1566)

RBR (Restaurant Buffet with Kitchen Mark 1) AJ41

1651	EH	1671	EH	1683	EH	1696	Fawley
1657	EH	1679	EH	1691	EH	1699	EH
1658	Fawley	1680	EH	1692	EH	1730	BT
1659	CS						

1683 CAROL

RSS (Restaurant Self Service Buffet Mark 2f) AN2F

1800 CS

RMB (Restaurant Miniature Buffet Mark 1) AN21

1813	EH	1840	CS	1859(99822)	BT	1861(99132)	CS
1823	NY	1842	EH	1860	CS	1863	EH
1832	EH	1851	RL				

RBR (Restaurant Buffet with Kitchen Mark 1) AJ41

1953 CP 1961 CS

SLSC (Sleeper Staff Coach Mark 1) AU51

2833(21270)CS 2834(21267)EH

Royal Train Coaches (Mark 3/*2) AT5

2903	ZN	2916(40512)	ZN	2919(40518)	ZNs	2922	ZN
2904	ZN	2917(40514)	ZN	2920*	ZN	2923	ZN
2915	ZN	2918(40515)	ZNs	2921*	ZN		

FO (First Open Mark 1) AD11

3058(975313)CS	3107 EH	3123 CP	3140 CP
3066(99566)EH	3110(99124)EH	3124 EH	3141 EH
3068(99568)EH	3112(99357)EHs	3125 EH	3143 CS
3069(99540)EH	3114 EHs	3127 EH	3144 EH
3093 CS	3115 BT	3128(99371)CS	3146 EH
3096(99827)BT	3119 EH	3131(99190)EHs	3147 EH
3097 EH	3120 EH	3132(99191)EHs	3148 EH
3098 EH	3121 EH	3133(99192)EHs	3149 EH
3100 EH	3122 CP	3136 CS	3150 BT

3058 FLORENCE
3093 PAULA
3128 VICTORIA
3136 DIANA
3143 PATRICIA

FO (First Open Mark 2d) AD1D

3174 CP	3182 CP	3186 i/u DY	3188 CS
3181 DE			

3174 GLAMIS
3181 TOPAZ
3182 WARWICK
3188 SOVEREIGN

FO (First Open Mark 2e) AD1E

3223 BO	3240 BO	3255 Fawley	3273 CP
3231 CS	3241 CS	3267 CP	3275 CP
3232 CD	3247 CP	3269 EH	

3223 DIAMOND
3231 BEN CRUACHAN
3240 SAPPHIRE
3247 CHATSWORTH
3267 BELVOIR
3273 ALNWICK
3275 HARLECH

FO (First Open Mark 2f) AD1F

3277 EH	3326 CS	3352 CS	3386 EH
3278 EH	3330 CP	3356 EH	3388 EH
3279 TO	3331 TO	3358 TO	3390 EH
3292 CE	3333 EH	3359 CS	3392 CS
3295 EH	3334 EH	3360 CS	3395 CS
3303 CEs	3336 EH	3362 CS	3397 MO
3304 EH	3338 EH	3364 MO	3399 EH
3309 CS	3340 EH	3366 KM	3400 TO
3312 CS	3344 EH	3368 Fawley	3408 CS
3313 CS	3345 EH	3374 KM	3414 EH
3314 EH	3348 CP	3375 EH	3416 CS
3318 TO	3350 CS	3379 EHs	3417 EH
3325 EH	3351 CS	3384 MO	3424 TO

3426	EH	3431	CS	3438	CS	3521	DE

3312 HELVELLYN
3330 BRUNEL
3348 GAINSBOROUGH
3356 TENNYSON
3364 SHAKESPEARE
3384 DICKENS
3390 CONSTABLE
3397 WORDSWORTH
3426 ELGAR

TSO/*SO (Tourist Standard Open Mark 1) AC21/*AD

3798	NY	4831(99824)	BT	4954(99326)	CS	5000	NY
3860	NY	4832(99823)	BT	4959	EH	5007	EHs
3872	NY	4836(99831)	BT	4960	CS	5008	EH
3948	NY	4856(99829)	BT	4973	CS	5009	EH
4198	NY	4905	CS	4984	CS	5023	EH
4252	NY	4927	EH	4986	EH	5027	EHs
4286	NY	4931(99329)	CS	4990	NY	5028(99830)	BT
4290	NY	4940	CS	4991	EH	5029	NY
4455	NY	4946	EH	4994	CS	5032(99194)	CS
4786*	NY	4949	EH	4996	CD	5035(99195)	CS
4817*	NY	4951	CS	4998	EH	5040	EH

TSO (Tourist Standard Open Mark 2) AC2Z

5125	BH	5179	TMs	5193	TMs	5212	TMs
5148	TMs	5183	TMs	5194	TMs	5216	CS
5157	TM	5186	TMs	5198	TM	5221	TMs
5171	CS	5191	TM	5200	CS	5222	CS
5177	TM						

5193 CLAN MACLEOD. 5212 CAPERKAILZIE.

SO (Standard Open Mark 2a) AD2Z

5229	CS	5237	CS	5239	CS	5249	CS
5236	CS						

TSO (Tourist Standard Open Mark 2a) AC2A

5276	EH	5322	EH	5350	CP	5412	BT
5278	CS	5331	Fawley	5366	EH	5419	CS
5292	EH	5341	EH	5386	Fawley		

TSO (Tourist Standard Open Mark 2b *2c) AC2B/*C

5453	SH	5478	SH	5487	SH	5569*	CS
5463	CS	5482	DE	5491	CS		

TSO (Tourist Standard Open Mark 2d) AC2D

5631	MH	5647	DE	5700	KM	5737	CS
5632	MH	5657	MH	5710	KM	5740	CS
5636 i/u	PM	5669	YK				

TSO (Tourist Standard Open Mark 2e) AC2E

5748	EH	5797	CS	5869	LM	5901	KM (ZK)
5756	CSu	5810	KM	5876	SH	5903	CS
5769	EH	5815	SH	5888	SH	5906	CD
5787	KM	5853	CF	5900	CS	5908	KM
5792	EH	5866	CD				

TSO (Tourist Standard Open Mark 2f) AC2F

5910	EH	5961	BH	6024	EH	6117	KM (ZG)
5912	CS	5964	ZG	6027	EH	6119	CFs
5913	LM	5965	CF	6029	SH	6122	KM (ZG)
5919	KM (ZK)	5971	KM (ZG)	6035	LM	6134	SH
5921	EH	5976	CF	6036	EH	6137	CF
5922	EH	5978	SH	6041	CS	6139	TO
5924	EH	5985	EH	6042	CP	6141	EH
5925	SH	5987	EH	6045	SH	6151	CS
5928	CS	5991	CS	6046	KM (ZK)	6152	EH
5929	EH	5995	KM (ZK)	6050	CS	6154	SH
5937	EH	5997	EH	6051	EH	6158	EH
5943	SH	5998	EH	6054	EH	6162	LM
5945	EH	6000	CS	6059	DE	6168	DE
5946	EH	6001	KM (ZG)	6064	KM (ZK)	6170	LM
5950	EH	6006	CP	6066	CFs	6173	KM (ZK)
5952	EH	6008	KM (ZG)	6067	EH	6175	SH
5954	EH	6009	SH	6073	SH	6176	EH
5955	EH	6012	CS	6103	CS	6177	EH
5958	SH	6013	LM	6110	EH	6179	SH
5959	EH	6021	CS	6115	CS	6183	CF
5960	DE	6022	CS				

GV (Generator Van Mark 1) **AX51**

6310(81448)EH 6311(92911)TT 6312(92925)CS 6313(92167)SL

ICS (Special Saloon) **AZ50**

6320(5033)SK Support Coach

(Desiro Barrier Vehicle) **NW51**

6321(96385)NN 6323(96387)NN 6324(96388)CP 6325(96389)NN
6322(96386)NN

HSBV (InterCity 125 Barrier Vehicle) **GS5**

6330	LA	6338	LA	6344	EC	6348	LA
6336	LA	6340	EC	6346	EC		

BV (InterCity 225 Barrier Vehicle) **AV5**

6352	BN	6354	BN	6358	BN	6359	BN
6353	BN	6355	BN				

BV (EMU Barrier Vehicle) **AW5**

6360	NL i/u	6364	CD	6376(975973)PG	6378(975971)PG
6361	NLu	6365	CD	6377(975975)PG	6379(975972)PG

HSBV (Barrier Vehicle InterCity 125) **GS5**

6392(92183)NL	6394(92906)EC	6396(92195)MA i/user	6398(92126)NL
6393(92196)EC	6395(92148)NL	6397(92190)NL	6399(92994)NL

TSOT (Standard Open Micro Buffet Mark 2c) **AG2C**

6528 CS

RLB (Restaurant Lounge Buffet First Mark 2f) **AN1F**

6700	IS	6703	IS	6705	IS	6707	IS
6701	IS	6704	IS	6706	IS	6708	IS
6702	IS						

RMBF (Miniature Buffet First Mark 2d) **AN2D**

6720(6652)EH 6722(6661)LM 6723(6662)CS 6724(6665)CS

(GWR First Saloon Mark 2) **AO10**

9004(99053)CS

BSOT (Brake Standard Open Mark 2) **AH2Z**

9101 TM 9104 CS

BSO (Brake Standard Open Mark 1) **AE21**

9267 NY 9274 NY

BSO (Brake Standard Open Mark 2) **AE2Z**

9391 CS 9392 CS

BSO (Brake Standard Open Mark 2a) **AE2A**

9419 KM 9428 KM

BSO (Brake Standard Open Mark 2c) **AE2C**

9440 CS 9448 DEs

BSO (Brake Standard Open Mark 2d) **AE2D**

9488 KM 9489 CS 9493 CS 9494 MH

BSO (Brake Standard Open Mark 2e) AE2E

9496	CS	9502	SL	9505	DEs	9508	KM (BH)
9497	DEs	9503	CFs	9506	MH	9509	LM
9500	DEs	9504	EH	9507	EH		

BSO (Brake Standard Open Mark 2f) AE2F

9520	EH	9524	LM	9527	EH	9537	EH
9521	CF	9525	KM (ZG)	9529	EH	9539	CF
9522	TO	9526	EH	9531	EH		

DBSO (Driving Brake Standard Open Mark 2f) AF2F

9704	ZG	9707	KM (ZG)	9710	ZG	9713	DE (ZG)
9705	KM (ZG)	9709	ZG	9711	TM		

BUO (Brake Unclassified Open Mark 2e) AE4E

9800(5751)IS	9803(5799)IS	9806(5840)IS	9809(5890)IS
9801(5760)IS	9804(5826)IS	9807(5851)IS	9810(5892)IS
9802(5772)IS	9805(5833)IS	9808(5871)IS	

RFM (Restaurant First Modular Mark 3a) AJ1G

10200	NC	10216	NC	10232	PZ	10247	NC
10201	LM	10217	LM	10233	LM	10249	CF
10202	LM	10219	PZ	10235	LM	10250	LM
10203	NC	10222	LM	10237	LM	10253	LM
10206	ZI	10223	NC	10240	LM	10256	Yoker (i/u)
10211	TO	10225	PZ	10241	ZI	10257	LM
10212	WB	10226	LM	10242	LM	10259	CF
10214	NC	10228	NC	10245	CS	10260	Yoker (i/u)
10215	LM	10229	NC	10246	CF		

GFW (Galley First Wheelchair Mark 3) AJ1G

10271(10236)AL	10272(10208)AL	10273(10230)AL	10274(10255)AL

RSB (Kitchen Standard Buffet Mark 4) AG2J

10300 BN
10301 BN
10302 BN
10303 BN
10304 BN
10305 BN
10306 BN
10307 BN
10308 BN
10309 BN
10310 BN
10311 BN
10312 BN
10313 BN
10315 BN
10317 BN
10318 BN
10319 BN
10320 BN
10321 BN
10323 BN
10324 BN
10325 BN
10326 BN
10328 BN
10329 BN
10330 BN
10331 BN
10332 BN
10333 BN

RMB (Standard Open with Miniature Buffet Mark 3A) AN2G

10401(12168)NC
10402(12010)NC
10403(12135)NC
10404(12068)NC
10405(12157)NC
10406(12020)NC

SLEP (Sleeper with Pantry Mark 3a) AU4G

10501 IS
10502 IS
10504 IS
10506 IS
10507 IS
10508 IS
10513 IS
10516 IS
10519 IS
10520 IS
10522 IS
10523 IS
10526 IS
10527 IS
10529 IS
10531 IS
10532 PZ
10534 PZ
10540 LM
10542 IS
10543 IS
10544 IS
10546 TO
10548 IS
10551 IS
10553 IS
10554 LM
10561 IS
10562 IS
10563 PZ
10565 IS
10580 IS
10584 PZ
10588 IS
10589 PZ
10590 PZ
10594 PZ
10596 LM
10597 IS
10598 IS
10600 IS
10601 PZ
10605 IS
10607 IS
10610 IS
10612 PZ
10613 IS
10614 IS
10616 PZ
10617 IS

SLE/•SLED (Sleeper Mark 3a) AS4G/•AQ4G

10647 LM
10648• IS
10650• IS
10666• IS
10675 IS
10680• IS
10681 LM
10682 LM
10683 IS
10688 IS
10689• IS
10690 IS
10693 IS
10699• IS
10701 LM
10703 IS
10706• IS
10709 LM
10710 LM
10714• IS
10718• IS
10719• IS
10722• IS
10723• IS
10729 CP
10731 LM
10734(2914)CP

10729 named CREWE. 10734 named BALMORAL

FO (First Open)*TSO Mark 3a

AD1G

11005	LM	11018	WB	11028	ZB	11039	TO
11006	LM	11019	ZB	11029*	AL	11044	LM
11007	WB	11021	ZI	11030	ZB	11046	ZB
11011	LM	11026	LM	11031*	AL	11048	WB
11013	LM	11027	LM	11033	LM	11054	ZB

FO (First Open Mark 3b)

AD1H

11066	NC	11075	NC	11085	NC	11094	NC
11067	NC	11076	NC	11087	NC	11095	NC
11068	NC	11077	NC	11088	NC	11096	NC
11069	NC	11078	NC	11089	LM	11097	LM
11070	NC	11079	LM	11090	NC	11098	NC
11072	NC	11080	NC	11091	NC	11099	NC
11073	NC	11081	NC	11092	NC	11100	NC
11074	ZI	11082	NC	11093	NC	11101	NC

FO (First Open Mark 4)

AD1J

11201	BN	11277(12408)BN	11284(12487)BN	11291(12535)BN
11219	BN	11278(12479)BN	11285(12537)BN	11292(12451)BN
11229	BN	11279(12521)BN	11286(12482)BN	11293(12536)BN
11237	BN	11280(12523)BN	11287(12527)BN	11294(12529)BN
11241	BN	11281(12418)BN	11288(12517)BN	11295(12475)BN
11244	BN	11282(12524)BN	11289(12528)BN	11298(12416)BN
11273	BN	11283(12435)BN	11290(12530)BN	11299(12532)BN

FOD (First Open Disabled Mark 4)

AD1J

11301(11215)BN	11309(11259)BN	11317(11223)BN	11324(11253)BN
11302(11203)BN	11310(11272)BN	11318(11251)BN	11325(11231)BN
11303(11211)BN	11311(11221)BN	11319(11247)BN	11326(11206)BN
11304(11257)BN	11312(11225)BN	11320(11255)BN	11327(11236)BN
11305(11261)BN	11313(11210)BN	11321(11245)BN	11328(11274)BN
11306(11276)BN	11314(11207)BN	11322(11228)BN	11329(11243)BN
11307(11217)BN	11315(11238)BN	11323(11235)BN	11330(11249)BN
11308(11263)BN	11316(11227)BN		

FO (First Open Mark 4) AD1J

11401(11214)BN
11402(11216)BN
11403(11258)BN
11404(11202)BN
11405(11204)BN
11406(11205)BN
11407(11256)BN
11408(11218)BN
11409(11262)BN
11410(11260)BN
11411(11240)BN
11412(11209)BN
11413(11212)BN
11414(11246)BN
11415(11208)BN
11416(11254)BN
11417(11226)BN
11418(11222)BN
11419(11250)BN
11420(11242)BN
11421(11220)BN
11422(11232)BN
11423(11230)BN
11424(11239)BN
11425(11234)BN
11426(11252)BN
11427(11200)BN
11428(11233)BN
11429(11275)BN
11430(11248)BN
11998(10314)BN
11999(10316)BN

TSO (Tourist Standard Open Mark 3a) AC2G

12005 NC
12008 ZB
12009 NC
12011 WB
12012 NC
12013 NC
12015 NC
12016 NC
12017 AL
12019 NC
12021 NC
12022 LM
12024 NC
12026 NC
12027 NC
12029 LM
12030 NC
12031 NC
12032 NC
12034 NC
12035 NC
12036 LM
12037 NC
12040 NC
12041 NC
12042 NC
12043 AL
12045 LM
12046 NC
12047 LM
12049 NC
12051 NC
12054 AL
12056 NC
12057 NC
12058 AL
12060 NC
12061 NC
12062 NC
12063 LM
12064 NC
12065 LM
12066 NC
12067 NC
12073 NC
12078 WB
12079 NC
12081 NC
12082 NC
12083 LM
12084 NC
12087 LM
12089 NC
12090 NC
12091 NC
12092 LM
12093 NC
12094 AL
12095 LM
12097 NC
12098 NC
12099 NC
12100 PZ
12101 LM
12103 NC
12104 AL
12105 NC
12107 NC
12108 NC
12109 NC
12110 NC
12111 NC
12114 NC
12115 NC
12116 NC
12118 NC
12119 AL
12120 NC
12122 WB
12124 AL
12125 NC
12126 NC
12129 NC
12130 NC
12132 NC
12133 WB
12134 LM
12137 NC
12138 WB
12139 NC
12141 NC
12142 LM
12143 NC
12144 LM
12146 NC
12147 NC
12148 NC
12150 NC
12151 NC
12153 NC
12154 NC
12156 LM
12158 BN
12159 NC
12160 LM
12161 PZ
12163 BN
12164 NC
12165 AL
12166 NC
12167 NC
12170 NC
12171 NC
12176(11064)CF
12177(11065)CF
12178(11071)CF
12179(11083)CF
12180(11084)CF
12181(11086)CF

TSOE (Tourist Standard Open - End Vehicle Mark 4) **AI2J**

12200 BN
12201 BN
12202 BN
12203 BN
12204 BN
12205 BN
12207 BN
12208 BN
12209 BN
12210 BN
12211 BN
12212 BN
12213 BN
12214 BN
12215 BN
12216 BN
12217 BN
12218 BN
12219 BN
12220 BN
12222 BN
12223 BN
12224 BN
12225 BN
12226 BN
12227 BN
12228 BN
12229 BN
12230 BN
12231 BN
12232 BN

TSOD (Tourist Standard Open - Disabled Access Mark 4) **AL2J**

12300 BN
12301 BN
12302 BN
12303 BN
12304 BN
12305 BN
12307 BN
12308 BN
12309 BN
12310 BN
12311 BN
12312 BN
12313 BN
12315 BN
12316 BN
12317 BN
12318 BN
12319 BN
12320 BN
12321 BN
12322 BN
12323 BN
12324 BN
12325 BN
12326 BN
12327 BN
12328 BN
12329 BN
12330 BN
12331(12531)BN

TSO (Tourist Standard Open Mark 4) **AC2J**

12400 BN
12401 BN
12402 BN
12403 BN
12404 BN
12405 BN
12406 BN
12407 BN
12409 BN
12410 BN
12411 BN
12414 BN
12415 BN
12417 BN
12419 BN
12420 BN
12421 BN
12422 BN
12423 BN
12424 BN
12425 BN
12426 BN
12427 BN
12428 BN
12429 BN
12430 BN
12431 BN
12432 BN
12433 BN
12434 BN
12436 BN
12437 BN
12438 BN
12439 BN
12440 BN
12441 BN
12442 BN
12443 BN
12444 BN
12445 BN
12446 BN
12447 BN
12448 BN
12449 BN
12450 BN
12452 BN
12453 BN
12454 BN
12455 BN
12456 BN
12457 BN
12458 BN
12459 BN
12460 BN
12461 BN
12462 BN
12463 BN
12464 BN
12465 BN
12466 BN
12467 BN
12468 BN
12469 BN
12470 BN
12471 BN
12472 BN
12473 BN
12474 BN
12476 BN
12477 BN
12478 BN
12480 BN
12481 BN
12483 BN
12484 BN
12485 BN
12486 BN
12488 BN
12489 BN
12513 BN
12514 BN
12515 BN
12518 BN
12519 BN
12520 BN
12522 BN
12526 BN
12533 BN
12534 BN
12538 BN

SO (Standard Open Mark 3a)

12601(110xx)	12606(12048)AL	12611(110xx)	12616(12127)AL
12602(12072)AL	12607(12038)AL	12612(110xx)	12617(12174)AL
12603(12053)AL	12608(12069)AL	12613(12173)AL	12618(12169)AL
12604(12131)AL	12609(12014)AL	12614(12145)AL	12619(12175)AL
12605(11040)AL	12610(12117)AL	12615(12059)AL	12620(110xx)

FK (First Corridor Mark 1/▫2A) **AA11/▫AA1A**

13227 EH	13230(99828)BT	13321(99316)CS	13440▫ CS
13229(99826)BT	13320 CSu		

FO (First Open Mark 1) **AD1B**

13508 BO

BFK (Brake First Corridor Mark 1) Support Coaches **AB11**

14007(99782) MERCATOR NY	14099 CS
14064(17064)CS	

CK (Corridor Mark 1) **AA31**

16156 NY

BFK (Brake First Corridor Mark 2a *1) x support coach **AB1A/*11/+Z**

17013* SH	17019x CS	17077 EH	17090 TM
17015* EH	17025x(99990)CS	17080(35516)CS	17096x SL
17018x TM	17056 EH		

17013 BOTAURUS. 17096 MERCATOR.

Generator/Service Couchette Mark 2b **AX5B**

17105(2905)EH

BFK (Brake First Corridor Mark 2d) **AB1D**

17156 DY i/user	17159 KM	17167Car No. 17167 CP	17168 CS

BUO (Brake Unclassified Open Mark 3b) **AE1H**

17173 PZ 17174 PZ 17175 PZ

BCK (Brake Composite Corridor Mark 1) x support coach **AB31**

21096 x(99080)NY
21100 NY
21232x CQ
21241 BT
21245 EH
21252 RL
21266 CS
21268x SH
21269 EH
21272 EH

BSK (Brake Standard Corridor Mark 1) x support coach **AB/·AR21**

35089 NY
35185 BT
35333x EH
35451(99313)HQ
35453x DI
35461x TM
35464x HQ
35465x SH
35467x KR
35469* EH
*used as generator van
35470x TM
35479x KR
35486(99405)xFife

BSK (Brake Standard Corridor Mark 2a x support coach **AB1A/·5C**

35508x BQ
35511(17130) Shildon (kitchen/generator coach)
35517x BQ
35518x SH

TSMB (HST Miniature Buffet Mark 3) **GN2G**

40101(42170)LA
40102(42223)LA
40103(42316)LA
40104(42254)LA
40105(42084)LA
40106(42162)LA
40107(42334)LA
40108(42314)LA
40109(42262)LA
40110(42187)LA
40111(42248)LA
40112(42336)LA
40113(42309)LA
40114(42086)LA
40115(42320)LA
40116(42147)LA
40117(42249)LA
40118(42338)LA
40119(42090)LA

TRFB (HST Restaurant First Buffet Mark 3) **GN1G**

40204 LA
40205 LA
40207 LA
40210 LA
40221 LA
40231 LA

TRSB (HST Restaurant Standard Buffet Mark 3) **GK2G**

40402 HT
40403 HT
40416 LM
40417 ZK
40419 LM
40424 HT
40425 ZK
40426 EC
40433 HT
40434 HT

TRFB (HST Restaurant First with Buffet Mark 3) **GK1G**

40700 NL
40701 EC
40702 EC
40703 LA
40704 EC
40705 EC
40706 EC
40707 LA
40708 EC
40710 LA
40711 EC
40713 LA

40715 LA
40716 LA
40718 LA
40720 EC
40721 LA
40722 LA
40723 LM
40724 ZK
40727 LA
40728 NL
40729 ZQ (NL)
40730 NL
40732 EC
40733 LA
40734 LA
40735 EC
40737 EC
40739 LA
40740 EC
40741 NL
40742 EC
40743 LA
40745 ZK
40746 NL
40748 EC
40749 NL
40750 EC
40751 NL
40752 LA
40753 NL
40754 NL
40755 LA
40756 NL
40757 LA

TRFB (HST Restaurant First with Buffet Mark 3) GL1G

40801(40427)LA
40802(40412)LA
40803(40418)LA
40804(40432)LA
40805(40420)EC
40806(40429)LA
40807(40435)LA
40808(40415)LA
40809(40414)LA
40810(40430)LA
40811(40411)LA

TRFB (HST Restaurant First with Buffet Mark 3) GL4G

40900(40422)LA
40901(40436)LA
40902(40423)LA
40903(40437)LA
40904(40401)LA

TF (HST Trailer First Mark 3) GH1G

41003 LA
41004 LA
41005 LA
41006 LA
41007 LA
41008 LA
41009 LA
41010 LA
41011 LA
41012 LA
41015 LA
41016 LA
41017 LA
41018 LA
41019 LA
41020 LA
41021 LA
41022 LA
41023 LA
41024 LA
41026 LA
41027 LA
41028 LA
41029 LA
41030 LA
41031 LA
41032 LA
41033 LA
41034 LA
41035 EC
41037 LA
41038 LA
41039 EC
41040 EC
41041 NL
41044 EC
41045 LA
41046 NL
41051 LA
41052 LA
41055 LA
41056 LA
41057 NL
41059 LA
41061 NL
41062 EC
41063 NL
41064 NL
41065 LA
41066 EC
41067 NL
41068 NL
41069 NL
41070 NL
41071 NL
41072 NL
41075 NL
41076 NL
41077 NL
41079 NL
41081 LA
41083 EC
41084 NL
41085 LA
41086 LA
41087 EC
41088 EC
41089 LA
41090 EC
41091 EC
41092 EC
41093 LA
41094 LA
41095 EC
41096 LA
41097 EC
41098 EC
41099 EC
41100 EC
41101 LA
41102 LA
41103 LA
41104 LA
41105 LA
41106 LA
41108 LA
41109 LA
41110 LA
41111 NL
41112 NL
41113 NL
41114 LA
41115 EC
41116 LA
41117 NL
41118 EC
41119 LA
41120 EC
41121 LA
41122 LA

41123 LA
41124 LA
41125 LA
41126 LA
41127 LA
41128 LA
41129 LA
41130 LA
41131 LA
41132 LA
41133 LA
41134 LA
41135 LA
41136 LA
41137 LA
41138 LA
41139 LA
41140 LA
41141 LA
41142 LA
41143 LA
41144 LA
41145 LA
41146 LA
41147 LA
41148 LA
41149 LA
41150 EC
41151 EC
41152 EC
41154 EC
41155 LA
41156 NL
41157 LA
41158 LA
41159 EC
41160 LA
41161 LA
41162 LA
41163 LA
41164 EC
41165 EC
41166 LA
41167 LA
41168 LA
41169 LA
41170(41001)EC
41176(42352)LA
41179(40505)LA
41180(40511)LA
41181(42282)LA
41182(42278)LA
41183(42274)LA
41184(42270)LA
41185(42313)EC
41186(42312)LA
41187(42311)LA
41189(42298)LA
41190(42088)EC
41191(42318)LA
41192(42246)LA
41193(11060)EC
41194(11016)EC
41195(11020)EC
41201(11045)HT
41202(11017)HT
41203(11038)HT
41204(11023)EC
41205(11036)HT
41206(11055)HT

TS (HST Trailer Standard Mark 3) GH2G

42003 LA
42004 LA
42005 LA
42006 LA
42007 LA
42008 LA
42009 LA
42010 LA
42012 LA
42013 LA
42014 LA
42015 LA
42016 LA
42019 LA
42021 LA
42023 LA
42024 LA
42025 LA
42026 LA
42027 LA
42028 LA
42029 LA
42030 LA
42031 LA
42032 LA
42033 LA
42034 LA
42035 LA
42036 EC
42037 EC
42038 EC
42039 LA
42040 LA
42041 LA
42042 LA
42043 LA
42044 LA
42045 LA
42046 LA
42047 LA
42048 LA
42049 LA
42050 LA
42051 EC
42052 EC
42053 EC
42054 LA
42055 LA
42056 LA
42057 EC
42058 EC
42059 EC
42060 LA
42061 LA
42062 LA
42063 EC
42064 EC
42065 EC
42066 LA
42067 LA
42068 LA
42069 LA
42070 LA
42071 LA
42072 LA
42073 LA
42074 LA
42075 LA
42076 LA
42077 LA
42078 LA
42079 LA
42080 LA
42081 LA
42083 LA
42085 LA
42087 LA
42089 LA
42091 EC
42092 LA
42093 LA
42094 LA
42095 LA
42096 LA
42097 EC
42098 LA
42099 LA
42100 NL
42101 LA
42102 LA
42103 LA
42104 EC
42105 LA
42106 EC
42107 LA
42108 LA
42109 EC
42110 EC
42111 NL
42112 NL
42113 NL
42115 LA
42116 EC
42117 EC
42118 LA
42119 NL
42120 NL
42121 NL
42122 EC
42123 EC
42124 NL
42125 EC

42126	LA
42127	EC
42128	EC
42129	LA
42130	EC
42131	NL
42132	NL
42133	NL
42134	EC
42135	NL
42136	NL
42137	NL
42138	LA
42139	NL
42140	NL
42141	NL
42143	LA
42144	LA
42145	LA
42146	EC
42148	NL
42149	NL
42150	EC
42151	NL
42152	NL
42153	NL
42154	EC
42155	NL
42156	NL
42157	NL
42158	EC
42159	EC
42160	EC
42161	EC
42163	EC
42164	NL
42165	NL
42166	LA
42167	LA
42168	LA
42169	LA
42171	EC
42172	EC
42173	LA
42174	LA
42175	LA
42176	LA
42177	LA
42178	LA
42179	EC
42180	EC
42181	EC
42182	EC
42183	LA
42184	LA
42185	LA
42186	EC
42188	EC
42189	EC
42190	EC
42191	EC
42192	EC
42193	EC
42194	NL
42195	LA
42196	LA
42197	LA
42198	EC
42199	EC
42200	LA
42201	LA
42202	LA
42203	LA
42204	LA
42205	EC
42206	LA
42207	LA
42208	LA
42209	LA
42210	EC
42211	LA
42212	LA
42213	LA
42214	LA
42215	EC
42216	LA
42217	LA
42218	LA
42219	EC
42220	NL
42221	LA
42222	LA
42224	LA
42225	NL
42226	EC
42227	NL
42228	EC
42229	NL
42230	NL
42231	LA
42232	LA
42233	LA
42234	EC
42235	EC
42236	LA
42237	EC
42238	EC
42239	EC
42240	EC
42241	EC
42242	EC
42243	EC
42244	EC
42245	LA
42247	LA
42250	LA
42251	LA
42252	LA
42253	LA
42255	LA
42256	LA
42257	LA
42258	LA
42259	LA
42260	LA
42261	LA
42263	LA
42264	LA
42265	LA
42266	LA
42267	LA
42268	LA
42269	LA
42271	LA
42272	LA
42273	LA
42275	LA
42276	LA
42277	LA
42279	LA
42280	LA
42281	LA
42283	LA
42284	LA
42285	LA
42286	EC
42287	LA
42288	LA
42289	LA
42290	EC
42291	LA
42292	LA
42293	LA
42294	LA
42295	LA
42296	LA
42297	LA
42299	LA
42300	LA
42301	LA
42302	LA
42303	LA
42304	LA
42305	LA
42306	EC
42307	EC
42308	LA
42310(41188)	LA
42315	LA
42317	LA
42319	LA
42321	LA
42322	EC
42323	EC
42325	LA
42326	EC
42327	NL
42328	NL
42329	NL
42330	EC
42331	NL
42332	LA
42333	LA
42335	EC
42337	NL
42339	NL
42340	EC
42341	NL
42342(44082)	EC
42343(44095)	LA
42344(44092)	LA
42345(44096)	LA
42346(41053)	LA
42347(41054)	LA
42348(41073)	LA
42349(41074)	LA
42350(41047)	LA
42351(41048)	LA
42353(41171)	LA
42354(41175)	EC

42355(41172)EC
42356(41173)LA
42357(41174)EC
42360(45084)LA
42361(44099)LA
42362(41178)LA
42363(41082)EC
42364(41080)LA
42365(41107)LA
42366(12007)EC
42367(12025)EC
42368(12028)EC
42369(12050)EC
42370(12086)EC
42371(12052)EC
42372(12055)EC
42373(12071)EC
42374(12075)EC
42375(12113)EC
42376(12085)EC
42377(12102)EC
42378(12123)EC
42379(41036)EC
42380(41025)EC
42381(41058)LA
42382(12128)LA
42383(12172)LA
42384(41078)NL
42385(41153)LA
42401(12149)HT
42402(12155)HT
42403(12033)HT
42404(12152)HT
42405(12136)HT
42406(12112)HT
42407(12044)HT
42408(12121)HT
42409(12088)HT

TS (HST Trailer Standard Mark 3) GK1G

42501(40744)LA
42502(40731)LA
42503(40712)LA
42504(40228)LA
42505(40714)LA
42506(40724)LA
42507(40209)LA
42508(40725)LA
42509(40736)LA
42510(40717)LA
42511(40709)LA
42512(40208)LA
42513(40738)LA
42514(40726)LA
42515(40747)LA

TGS (HST Trailer Guard's Standard Mark 3) GJ2G

44000 LA
44001 LA
44002 LA
44003 LA
44004 LA
44005 LA
44007 LA
44008 LA
44009 LA
44010 LA
44011 LA
44012 EC
44013 LA
44014 LA
44015 LA
44016 LA
44017 EC
44018 LA
44019 EC
44020 LA
44021 EC
44022 LA
44023 LA
44024 LA
44025 LA
44026 LA
44027 NL
44028 LA
44029 LA
44030 LA
44031 EC
44032 LA
44033 LA
44034 LA
44035 LA
44036 LA
44037 LA
44038 LA
44039 LA
44040 LA
44041 NL
44042 LA
44043 LA
44044 NL
44045 EC
44046 NL
44047 NL
44048 NL
44049 LA
44050 EC
44051 NL
44052 EC
44054 NL
44055 LA
44056 EC
44057 EC
44058 EC
44059 LA
44060 LA
44061 EC
44063 EC
44064 LA
44065 HT
44066 LA
44067 LA
44068 LA
44069 LA
44070 NL
44071 NL
44072 EC
44073 EC
44074 LA
44075 EC
44076 LA
44077 EC
44078 LA
44079 LA
44080 EC
44081 LA
44083 LA
44085 NL
44086 LA
44088 HT
44089 HT
44090 LA
44091 LA
44093 LA
44094 EC
44097 LA
44098 EC
44100 PM
44101 LA

TCC (Trailer Composite Catering Mark 3) GH3G

45001(12004)EC
45002(12106)EC
45003(12076)EC
45004(12077)EC
45005(12080)EC

RK (Kitchen Mark 1) AK51

80041(1690)EH 80042(1646)EH

BG (Courier Van Mark 1) x support coach NN51

80204x SH 80217x(35299)CS 80220x NY

DVT (Driving Van Trailer Mark 3b) NZAH

82101	CG	82113	LM	82125	LM	82139	NC
82102	NC	82114	NC	82126	WB	82140	LM
82103	NC	82115	ZN	82127	NC	82141	LM
82104	LM	82116	LM	82129	LB	82143	NC
82105	NC	82118	NC	82132	NC	82145	LB
82106	LM	82120	LM	82133	NC	82146	TO
82107	NC	82121	NC	82136	NC	82148	LM
82110	LM	82122	LM	82137	LM	82150	LM
82111	LB	82123	LM	82138	LM	82152	NC
82112	NC	82124	LB				

DVT (Driving Van Trailer Mark 4) NZAJ

82200	BN	82208	BN	82216	BN	82225	BN
82201	BN	82209	BN	82217	BN	82226	BN
82202	BN	82210	BN	82218	BN	82227	BN
82203	BN	82211	BN	82219	BN	82228	BN
82204	BN	82212	BN	82220	BN	82229	BN
82205	BN	82213	BN	82222	BN	82230	BN
82206	BN	82214	BN	82223	BN	82231	BN
82207	BN	82215	BN	82224	BN	SKYFALL	

DVT (Driving Van Trailer Mark 3b) NZAH

Converted to work push-pull with class 67

82301(82117)AL	82303(82135)AL	82305(82134)AL	82307(82131)CF
82302(82151)AL	82304(82130)AL	82306(82144)CF	82308(82108)CF

BG (Non-Gangwayed Van Mark 1) NB5

84519 CDu

BG (Gangwayed Van Brake Mark 1) 100/110mph *NE51/NH51

92111	CDu	92146	HQ	92159	CS	92303	EH

PSG (Gangwayed Van Mark 1) 100mph NF51

92400 CD

BG (Gangwayed Van Brake Mark 1) 100/110mph NE51/NH51

92901	WB i/user	92908	CSu	92929	CDu	92936	EH
92904(99554)	CP						

GUV (General Utility Van Mark 1 Vacuum Brake) 90mph NJ50

93219 i/user 024787 grounded at Nottingham
93425 i/user 041947 at Ilford
93714 i/user 061223 at Oxford Station
93975 i/user 042154 at Ipswich Upper Yard

GUV (Super General Utility Van fitted roller shutter doors) NK50

All officially withdrawn and awaiting disposal but on occasions temporary reinstated to traffic.

94101	i/user	CS	94147	(95147)	MO	94195	(95355)	BS	94214	(95374)	MH
94103	(95103)	Cardiff	94153	(95153)	WE	94196	(95356)	MH	94217	(93131)	MH
94104	(95104)	TW	94160	(95160)	MH	94197	(95357)	BS	94221	(93905)	MO
94106	(95106)	MH	94166	(95166)	BS	94199	(95359)	MH	94222	(93474)	MH
94116	(95116)	TY	94170	(95170)	MH	94207	(95367)	TW	94224	(93273)	CD
94121	i/user	TO	94176	(95176)	BS	94208	(95368)	TW	94225	(93849)	MH
94135	i/user	OX	94177	(95177)	TW	94209	(95369)	Cardiff	94227	(93585)	TE
94137	(95137)	MO	94192	(95352)	MO	94213	(95373)	MO	94229	(93720)	MH

94135 internal user 061061 at Oxford Station.

PCV (Propelling Control Vehicle) converted from class 307 NA50

94302	(75124)	TY	94311	(75105)	WE	94323	(75110)	TY	94336	(75031)	TY
94303	(75131)	TY	94313	(75129)	WE	94326	(75123)	TY	94337	(75029)	WE
94304	(75107)	MH	94316	(75108)	TW	94331	(75022)	Cardiff	94338	(75008)	WE
94306	(75112)	TY	94317	(75117)	TW	94332	(75011)	TY	94340	(75012)	CD
94307	(75127)	Cardiff	94318	(75115)	Cardiff	94333	(75016)	TY	94343	(75027)	MH
94308	(75125)	MH	94322	(75111)	MH	94335	(75032)	TY	94344	(75014)	TW
94310	(75119)	WE									

All officially withdrawn and awaiting disposal

BG (Super Brake Van 100/*+110mph fitted roller shutter doors) NB/*NI/+NQ

All officially withdrawn and awaiting disposal except 94515 & 94538

94400	(92954)	Cardiff	94434	(92584)	TY	94497	(92717)	MO	94529	(92252)	CD
94401	(92224)	MH	94435	(92134)	TW	94498	(92555)	MH	94530	(94409)	MO
94406	(92956)	MH	94438	i/user	TT	94499	(92577)	CD	94531	(94456)	TY
94408	(92981)	TY	94440	(92645)	MO	94501	(92725)	TW	94532	(94489)	LM
94410	(92941)	WE	94445	(92615)	WE	94504	(92748)	TY	94534	(94430)	MO
94411	(92997)	Cardiff	94451	(92257)	WE	94512	(92582)	TY	94536	(94491)	MO
94412	(92945)	MO	94458	(92974)	Cardiff	94514	(92122)	MO	94538	(94426)	EH
94413	(92236)	MO	94462	(92270)	CD	94515	(92513)	EH	94539	(92302)	MH
94416	(92746)	MO	94463	(92995)	TY	94517	(92243)	CD	94540	(92860)	TJ
94420	(92263)	MH	94470	(92113)	TW	94518	(92258)	MO	94541	(92316)	MO
94422	(92651)	TW	94479	(92132)	TW	94519	(92916)	MO	94542	(92330)	TY
94423	(92914)	BS	94481	(92641)	Cardiff	94520	(92510)	TY	94543	(92389)	MO
94427	(92754)	WE	94482	(92639)	MH	94521	(92917)	CD	94544	(92345)	MH
94428	(92166)	MO	94488	(92105)	CD	94522	(92907)	TY	94545	(92329)	TE
94429	(92232)	TE	94490	(92606)	MH	94525	(92229)	TY	94546	(92804)	TY
94431	(92604)	MH	94492	(92721)	WE	94526	(92518)	TY	94547	(92392)	MH
94432	(92999)	MO	94494		**	94527	(92728)	TY	94548	(92344)	TY
94433	(92643)	MH	94495	(92755)	TY	94528	(92267)	MO			

*94514/25/26/30/34/36. +94504/515/519/520/527/531/532/538. **94494 i/user 083602 at Three Bridges.

CCT (Covered Van Mark 1)

94752 i/user 083439 at Wimbledon Depot

GUV (General Utility Van 100 mph) NO50

95199(93141)BH
Owned by AC Loco Group

PCV (Propelling Control Vehicle) NA50

95300(94300)MH 95301(94301)MH

Note:- Propelling controls isolated.

BG (BAA Container Van) NR51

Both officially withdrawn and awaiting disposal.

95400 MH 95410 MH

Super GUV (General Utility Van fitted Roller Shutter Doors) NO50

All officially withdrawn and awaiting disposal

95727 (95127) WE 95754 (95154) TY 95761 (95161) WE 95763 (95163) BS

GUV (Motorail Van 100/*110mph) NX50/*NP50

96100* i/user at TM 96139 i/user at MA 96175 CS

Eurostar Night Stock Generator Van

96371(6371)WB 96373(6373)LM 96374(6374)ZB 96375(6375)LM
96372(6372)LM

Eurostar Barrier

96380(6380)TI 96381(6381)TI 96383(6383)TI 96384(6384)TI

GUV (Car Carrier) NV5A

96602(96150)RU(AW) 96604(96156)CF 96606(96213)RU(AW) 96608(96216)RU(AW)
96603(96155)CF 96605(96157)RU 96607(96215)RU 96609(96217)RU(AW)

Translator Vehicle (used for haulage of EMU stock) NY50

ADB975864(3849)PO ADB975875(34643) ADB975978(1025)ZB ADB977087(34971)
ADB975867(1006)PO ADB975974(1030)ZB

975974 Paschar. 975978 Perpetiel.

Translator/Barrier Vehicle

DB977942(80251)TO DB977943(80252)TO DB977948(94025)WB DB977949(94028)WB

SERVICE STOCK (RTC Derby), Serco Railtest/DeltaRail and Network Rail

NUMBER CARRIED			
1205	(6438)	Network Rail	ZA
1256	(3296)	Network Rail Staff Coach	ZA
5981		Network Rail Staff Coach	ZA
6260	(92116)	Network Rail Generator Van	WR
6261	(92988)	Network Rail Generator Van	ZA
6262	(92928)	Network Rail Generator Van	ZA
6263	(92961)	Network Rail Generator Van	ZA
6264	(92923)	Network Rail Generator Van	ZA
9481		Network Rail Staff Coach	ZA
9516		Network Rail Support Coach	ZA
9523		Network Rail Support Coach	ZA
9701	(9528)	Network Rail	ZA
9702	(9510)	Network Rail	ZA
9703	(9517)	Network Rail	ZA
9708	(9530)	Network Rail	ZA
9714	(9536)	Network Rail	ZA
68501	(9102)	Network Rail De-icer	ZA*
68504	(9105)	Network Rail De-icer	ZA*
68505	(9106)	Network Rail De-icer	ZA*
72612	(6156)	Test Train Coach	ZA
72616	(6007)	Test Train Coach	ZA
72630	(6094)	Test Train Coach	ZA
72631	(6096)	Test Train Coach	ZA
72639	(6070)	Test Train Coach	ZA
80211	(35296)	Network Rail Support Coach	ZAu
92114		Network Rail Support Coach	ZA
TRAN 93500		Serco Railtest PFA Flat Wagon	ZAu
CC 99019	(1870)	Network Rail Track Assessment Coach	YKu
ADB 971001	(94150)	Network Rail Support Coach	BS
ADB 971002	(94190)	Network Rail Support Coach	WA
ADB 971003	(94191)	Network Rail Support Coach	BS
ADB 971004	(94168)	Network Rail Support Coach	Worksop
975025	(60755)	For use with Network Rail (CAROLINE)	ZA
DB 975081	(35313)	Network Rail Structure Guaging Coach	ZA
ADB 975087	(34289)	Network Rail Support Coach	Worksop
975091	(34615)	Network Rail Overhead Line Equipment Test Coach	ZA
DB 975280	(21263)	Network Rail Structure Guaging Coach	ZA
ADB 975290	(13396)	Serco Railtest Test Car 6	ZG
ADB 975397	(35386)	Serco Railtest Test Car 2	ZA
ADB 975464	(35171)	Network Rail Support Coach	WA
975471	(34543)	Network Rail Support Coach	ZA
ADB 975477	(35108)	Network Rail Support Coach	Worksop
ADB 975486	(34100)	Network Rail Support Coach	WA
975814	(41000)	Network Rail Conference Vehicle	EC
975984	(40000)	Network Rail Generator Car, New Measurement Train	EC
977868	(5846)	Network Rail Radio Signal Survey Coach	ZA
DB977869	(5858)	Network Rail Snowtrain Support Coach	IS
ADB 977905	(80215)	Serco Railtest Brake Force Runner	ZG
977969	(2906)	Network Rail Strategic Use	ZG

RDB 977974	(5854)	DeltaRail Laboratory Coach 5	ZA
977983	(72503)	Electrification Measurement Coach Coach	ZA
977984	(40501)	Network Rail Instrument Test Car 4	EC
DB 977985	(72715)	Network Rail Support Coach	ZA
DB 977986	(99664)	Network Rail Support Coach	ZA
977989	(10536)	Staff Mess Coach	ZA
DB 977990	(92937)	Network Rail Tool Van	ZA
977993	44053	Test Train Coach for new measurement train	EC
977994	44087	Test Train Coach	EC
977995	40619	Test Train Coach	EC
977997	(72613)	Radio Survey Coach	ZA
99666	(3250)	Ultrasonic Test Coach for Network Rail	ZA
DB 999508		Serco Railtest Track Recording Coach	ZA
999550		High Speed Track Recording Laboratory Coach	ZA
999602	62483	Ultrasonic Test Train Coach for Network Rail	ZA
999605	62482	Ultrasonic Test Train Coach for Network Rail	ZA
999606	62356	Ultrasonic Test Train Coach for Network Rail	ZA
	62384	Ultrasonic Test Train Coach for Network Rail	ZA

* Normally found at Tonbridge West Yard when not in use on de-icing duty

CHARTER/SUPPORT COACHES
Not listed in capital stock

The following pages list coaches that may carry a 99xxx number which is coloured yellow. This can be found attached to the solebar and the pass date can be found painted in a white triangle also on the solebar. It must be noted that some vehicles listed may no longer carry the 99xxx number and may have carried a different number at some stage.

CN	Carriage & Traction Group
FS	Flying Scotsman Services
GS	Great Scottish & Western Railway Co.
MN	Merchant Navy Locomotive Preservation Society
NM	National Railway Museum
NY	North Yorkshire Moors Railway
RA	Railfilms (Atlantic & North Western)
SH	Scottish Highland Railway Co. (Queen of Scots)
SVR	Severn Valley Railway
VS	Venice Simplon Orient Express (South)
	Venice Simplon Orient Express (Northern Belle)
VT	Vintage Trains (Birmingham Railway Museum)
WC	West Coast Railway Co.
MPXX	Miscellaneous Owners – Stored/Non Operational

Numbers & Name carried			Type Comment	Codes	
99035	35322		BSK, Mark 1	WC	CS
99040	21232		BCK, Mark 1 (support coach)		SK
99041	35476		BSK, Mark 1 (support coach)	WC	CS
99121	3105	JULIA	FO, Mark 1	WC	CS
99122	3106	ALEXANDRA	FO, Mark 1	WC	CS
99125	3113	JESSICA	FO, Mark 1	WC	CS
99127	3117	CHRISTINA	FO, Mark 1	WC	CS
99128	3130	PAMELA	FO, Mark 1	WC	CS
99131	1999	VICTORY Dining Car 2	LNER, prototype first	GS	CS
99141	17041		BFK, Mark 2 (support coach)		BQ
99241	35449	ELIZABETH	BSK, Mark 1 (support coach)		BQ
99302	13323		FK, Mark 1	WC	CSu
99304	21256		BCK, Mark 1	WC	CS
99311	1882		RMB, Mark 1	WC	CS
99312	35463		BSK, Mark 1 (support coach)	WC	CS
99317	3766		TSO, Mark 1	WC	CS
99318	4912		TSO, Mark 1	WC	CS
99319	17168	(14168)	BFK, Mark 2d	WC	CSs
99323	5704		TSO, Mark 2d	WC	CS
99324	5714		TSO, Mark 2d	WC	CS
99327	5044		TSO, Mark 1	WC	CS
99328	5033		TSO, Mark 1	WC	CS
99347	347	CAR NO. 347	Pullman Parlour Second	WC	CS
99348	348	CAR NO. 348	Pullman Parlour Second	WC	CS
99349	349	CAR NO. 349	Pullman Parlour Second	VT	CS
99350	350	CAR NO. 350	Pullman Parlour Second	WC	CS
99352	352	CAR NO. 352	Pullman Parlour Second	WC	CS
99353	353	CAR NO. 353	Pullman Parlour Second	VT	TM
99354	354	THE HADRIAN BAR	Pullman Second Bar	WC	CS
99361	335	CAR NO. 335	Pullman Parlour	VT	TM
99513		WR 2511			DI
99530	301	PERSEUS	Pullman Parlour First	VS	SL
99531	302	PHOENIX	Pullman Parlour First	VS	SL
99532	308	CYGNUS	Pullman Parlour First	VS	SL
99534	245	IBIS	Pullman Kitchen First	VS	SL
99535	213	MINERVA	Pullman Brake First	VS	SL
99536	254	ZENA	Pullman Parlour First	VS	SL
99537	280	AUDREY	Pullman Kitchen First	VS	SL
99539	255	IONE	Pullman Kitchen First	VS	SL
99541	243	LUCILLE	Pullman Kitchen First	VS	SL
99543	284	VERA	Pullman Kitchen First	VS	SL
99545	35466	BAGGAGE CAR NO.11	BSK, Mark 1	VS	SL
99546	281	GWEN	Pullman Kitchen First	VS	SL
99670	546	CITY OF MANCHESTER	Pullman Parlour First	WC	CS
99671	548	GRASMERE	Pullman Parlour First	WC	CS
99672	549	BASSENTHWAITE	Pullman Parlour First	WC	CS
99673	550	RYDAL WATER	Pullman Parlour First	WC	CS
99674	551	BUTTERMERE	Pullman Parlour First	WC	CS

99675	552	ENNERDALE WATER	Pullman Parlour First	WC	CS
99676	553	CRUMMOCK WATER	Pullman Parlour First	WC	CS
99677	586	DERWENTWATER	Pullman Brake First	WC	CS
99678	504	ULLSWATER	Pullman Kitchen First	WC	CS
99679	506	WINDERMERE	Pullman Kitchen First	WC	CS
99680	17102		BFK, Mark 2a (attendants car)	WC	CS
99710	18767	(25767)	SK, Mark 1	WC	SH
99712	18893	(25893)	SK, Mark 1	WC	CS
99716	18808	(25808)	SK, Mark 1	WC	SH
99718	18862	(25862)	SK, Mark 1	WC	SH
99721	18756	(25756)	SK, Mark 1	WC	SH
99722	18806	(25806)	SK, Mark 1	WC	CS
99723	35459		BSK, Mark 1 (support coach)	WC	CS
99750	21661	(KWVR 22) (DE902179)	NER 1661 Clerestory Saloon		HQ
99792	17019		BFK, Mark 1		NY
99886	35407	86 Service Car No.1	BSK, Mark 1	WC	CS
99887	2127		SLF, Mark 1	GS	CSs
99953	35468		BSK, Mark 1 (support for 60800)	NR	YK
99961	324	STATE CAR No.1 (AMBER)	Pullman Parlour First	GS	CS
99962	329	STATE CAR No.2 (PEARL)	Pullman Parlour First	GS	CS
99963	331	STATE CAR No.3 (TOPAZ)	Pullman Parlour First	GS	CS
99964	313	STATE CAR No.4 (FINCH)	Pullman Kitchen First	GS	CS
99965	319	OBSERVATION CAR	Pullman Kitchen First	GS	CS
99966	34525		Generator Van	GS	CS
99967	317	DINING CAR No.1 (RAVEN)	Pullman Kitchen First	GS	CS
99968	10541	STATE CAR No.5	SLEP, Mark 3a	GS	CS
99969	10556	SERVICE CAR/Generator	SLEP, Mark 3a	GS	CS
99993	5067	LMS CLUB CAR	TSO, Mark 1	RA	CS
	889202	BAGGAGE CAR NO.8	Ferry Van (used for stores)	VS	SLu

NREA would like to express their thanks to all companies and individuals who have supplied information for this edition of Spotters Companion.

MANCHESTER TRAM CLASS 185 . 3061